THE LA LAWBOOK

BY EDWARD GROSS

Books for the entertainment buyer

PIONEER

ALSO BY THE SAME AUTHOR:

- •Trek: The Lost Years
- •The Unofficial Tale of Beauty and the Beast
- •The Making of the Next Generation
- •The 25th Anniversary Odd Couple Companion
- •Secret File: The Making of Wiseguy
- •Bruce Lee: Fists of Fury
- •Paul McCartney: 20 Years On His Own
- •The Dark Shadows Tribute Book (with James Van Hise)
- •The Secret of Michael J. Fox's Success
- •The Films of Eddie Murphy
- •Top Gun: The Films of Tom Cruise
- •Rocky and the Films of Sylvester Stallone
- •Growing Up in the Sixties: The Wonder Years
- •The Fab Films of the Beatles

Designed and Edited by Hal Schuster with the assistance of Bob Garsson

Library of Congress Cataloging-in-Publication Data
Edward Gross, 1960—
        LA Lawbook

        1.   LA Lawbook (television)
    I. Title

Published by Pioneer Books, Inc., 5715 N. Balsam Rd., Las Vegas, NV, 89130.

First Printing, 1991

To my wife, Eileen and Thursday nights at 10

EDWARD GROSS has written for a variety of publications, including PREMIERE, STARLOG, COMICS SCENE, NEW YORK/LONG ISLAND NIGHTLIFE, FANGORIA and CINEFANTASTIQUE. He is the author of TREK: THE LOST YEARS, THE UNOFFICIAL TALE OF BEAUTY AND THE BEAST, THE MAKING OF THE NEXT GENERATION, THE ODD COUPLE COMPANION, SECRET FILE: THE MAKING OF A WISEGUY and PAUL McCARTNEY: 20 YEARS ON HIS OWN. In addition, he co-authored the story for an episode of ABC's SUPERCARRIER and his first screenplay is scheduled to go into production later this year. He lives on Long Island, New York with his wife Eileen and their son, Teddy.

LA LAWBOOK

INTRODUCTION

Perry Mason never lost a case!

Okay, Masonites, put down your pens. Let's concede that Perry did lose in the courtroom, but it was only three times and they can hardly be called losses in the traditional sense. There were extenuating circumstances in each situation and two of those three losses were later overturned.

Since the time of Monsieur Mason, television has experimented with more law shows, resulting in such efforts as *The Defiant Ones, Owen Marshall, The New Perry Mason* (Monte Markham inheriting Raymond Burr's case load) and a series of very successful Perry Mason TV movies. The one thing that most of them have in common is their standard "television" approach. The bad guys are just plain bad, the good guys beyond reproach and any crisis, no matter how severe, is wrapped up in 60 minutes.

It wasn't until Steven Bochco, generally considered to be the man who revolutionized the medium during the 1980s, passed the prime time bar that the law show came into its own. What *Hill Street Blues* did for cops, the Bochco/Terry Louise Fisher-created *L.A. Law* did for lawyers.

Unlike its predecessors, *L.A. Law* is an ensemble drama that provides the audience with a number of unique actors who must work together under the umbrella of their law firm, McKenzie-Brackman. From the first episode, it was obvious that this was a show with a difference. Here the line between right and wrong was more hazy than on other series; the characters are vested with a variety of emotions, opinions and passions. Additionally, *L.A. Law* spends as much time on the private lives of its protagonists as it does on the professional, and the issues they deal with aren't so clear-cut.

Mistakes are made, compromises given and the battle for justice wages on. The important thing to note, and this is probably the most significant difference between *L.A. Law* and other genre shows, is that the good guys do lose cases, some are better lawyers than others and oftentimes a victory in court is no cause for celebration.

This is an adult series, with flesh and blood human beings and scripts that don't find it necessary to pull punches. District Attorney Grace Van Owen is shot by a member of a gang whose leader she put away for life. Does she purchase a gun to protect herself from further retribution?

McKenzie-Brackman's Ann Kelsey is told by her client that he's a cold-blooded killer. She has a choice: tell the authorities and betray attorney-client privilege, remain quiet and do nothing or quit the legal practice and let the chips fall where they may. No easy decision to be sure.

Arnold Becker handles the divorces of many a beautiful woman. How doe he fight the temptation to sleep with them and possibly compromise his position? He doesn't, and has slept with many of them over the past five years.

Victor Sifuentes is thrust into a case defending a killer who has all but admitted his guilt. Does he roll over and play dead or defend his client as his responsibility as an attorney calls for?

Leland McKenzie allows the power base of the firm to shift, and his choices are clear-cut: reassert himself in order to gain control again or back down, a tired and broken man.

Simply put, these are not the typical dilemmas that prime time heroes find themselves facing week in and week out. Additionally, in the tradition of *Hill Street Blues,* many of the cases being dealt with are handled in individual episodes, but there are diverse interwining thematic elements that continue from week to week, creating a tapestry that spreads out over the course of an entire season.

Throughout the pages of the *L.A. Lawbook,* you'll meet each of the actors making up the ensemble and experience the entire run of the series through an episode guide that covers the very first episode through the early portion of the fifth season.

L.A. Law is the recipient of numerous awards for its outstanding quality. It's our hope that this volume will serve as the perfect companionpiece for the series itself.

Read on, for court is in session.

Edward Gross

January, 1991

Assistant DA Grace Van Owen, portrayed by Sandra Dey, meets her match in lawyer Lee Atkins, portrayed by James Earl Jones.

PLAYER dossiers

LA LAW is one of the most complex television series ever to air on American television, certainly on American network television. It is a blend of courtroom drama and soap opera involving a huge ensemble cast. A scorecard of the various players is almost essential to understanding the stories. Forewith is a guide to the many characters and the fine actors and actresses who play them.

The cast of LA LAW.
(Front row, left to right) Michele Greene, Richard Dysart and Blair Underwood
(Second row, left to right) Michael Tucker, Susan Ruttan, Susan Dey and Harry Hamlin
(Third row, left to right) Jill Eikenberry, Corbin Bersen and Alan Rachins
(Last row, left to right) Larry Drake and Jimmy Smits

HARRY HAMLIN
(MICHAEL KUZAK)

"Kuzak is the dark prince of the ensemble. There's a potential for explosiveness. It's his emotional remoteness that's compelling."
—Jacob Epstein, Writer
(As told to *TV Guide*)

As trial lawyer and McKenzie-Brackman's head of litigation Michael Kuzak, Harry Hamlin has done a fascinating job over the last five years, creating a realistic, multi-faceted character that has played a large part in making *L.A. Law* such a phenomenal success.

Through the course of the series we've witnessed the gradual growth of this character, slowly (considerably more slowly than the rest of the ensemble) coming to understand that which drives him. Kuzak is a man who believes in the system he represents, although he's often frustrated with its mechanics, particularly when an innocent person is caught up in its gears. Seldom will he turn down a client and, in fact, has gone to jail on contempt charges for several of them when he's refused to accept the court's handling of their cases.

On the personal side, we've watched the development and eventual demise of his relationship with Grace Van Owen. He slowly allowed himself to open up to her (we say slowly due to the fact that months after they began dating she accidentally discovered he had once been married), shared his emotions and closed them off again when they began drifting. Most recently, he experienced jealousy and pain when she became involved with fellow lawyer Victor Sifuentes, with no apparent chance of them (Grace and Michael) ever getting back together.

"Here was a very interesting piece of work that would allow me to stretch in a lot of subtle ways," Hamlin said of *L.A. Law*. "I got excited by the potential of exploring this one character over a long period of time. The man I'm playing is in the process of discovering himself and making decisions about being upwardly mobile while still observing justice and honor in his profession.

"To get a sense of realism," he added, "I went down and watched court proceedings."

The beginning of Hamlin's professional career can be traced back to 1978, when he completed a two-season run as Alan Strang in the American Conservatory Theatre production of *Equus*. So effective was his performance that he was awarded a Fullbright Scholarship to study Shakespeare in London. En route, however, he

was asked by Warner Brothers to read off-camera lines for a pair of actresses testing for a Stanley Donen film entitled *Movie, Movie*. Apparently he was quite good in his reading of those lines, because Donen cast him as boxer Joey Popchick in one segment of that film's two stories.

In 1982, he portrayed Hamlet on stage with Princeton's McCarter Theatre Company. He followed with the role of Perseus in Ray Harryhausen's *Clash of the Titans,* which featured an all-star cast but was not much of a film. He followed with *Making Love,* a gay romantic story, and such films as *Blue Skies Again* and *King of the Mountain.*

His television credits include the mini-series *Studs Lonigan, Space* and *Master of the Game,* as well as the original HBO film for cable, *Laguna Heat.* At the time of this writing, there are rumblings that his fifth season on *L.A. Law* will be his last. Whether this is true or not, he remains highly enthusiastic regarding the series itself, exemplified by the reaction of himself and the rest of the cast when the latest script arrives on the set.

"People literally dive on it," he laughed. "And I'm not just talking about actors. Everyone from the grip to the gaffer is buried in that script to find out what happens next. They're that good."

SUSAN DEY
(GRACE VAN OWEN)

As Grace Van Owen, Susan Dey has had a great opportunity to try each and every aspect of representing the law, which has aided in the growth of the character.

When *L.A. Law* began, Van Owen was a member of the district attorney's office. Some time later she went into private practice, until a gangster who wanted her to represent his nephew was shot to death in front of her. This led Grace back to the D.A.'s office. Then she was made a judge, but the clear-cut decisions of law that had to be made by her were overwhelming and she voiced her feelings that she wouldn't be long for the bench. Finally, when Leland McKenzie was told that Michael Kuzak was leaving the firm to join his sick father in New York, he went to Van Owen and convinced her to join McKenzie-Brackman as the new head of litigation. She accepted.

While all of this was going on, the character's backdrop was the ups and downs of her extremely sexually-oriented relationship with Kuzak. It seemed as though the two of them would eventually be married but they abruptly broke up. We've seen how the emotional turmoil of her particular vocation has taken its toll, resulting, at one point, in her slipping into alcoholism and drug abuse, and the way that this problem impacted on her relationship with Kuzak.

"(When I read for the part), right away I knew it was a part worth fighting for," Dey, who portrayed Laurie Partridge on *The Partridge Family* has related. "It's rare to come across a role on a series that (is) worth fighting for. One of the reasons I love my character is because I can give her my neuroses. Gracie has a side of vulnerability in her that was never exposed. For her to admit 'I love you' (to Kuzak) was the hardest thing in the world. It meant, 'I need you, I trust you.' She's going through what so many women are going through. D.A. is a tough position to put a woman in. I can stand in the courtroom asking for the death sentence, and part of my homework is to be a *woman* doing that. I love playing a powerful woman who is also sexual.

"I'm fascinated with how Grace operates in the court. She really commands the room—it's *'I'm right.'* But what happens when she's in the grocery line and someone cuts in front of her? I'd like to take those elements in her and test them on the streets."

In addition to her well known role on *The Partridge Family,* she has starred in such television productions as *Emerald Point, N.A.S., Little Women, Mary Jane*

Harper Cried Last Night, Cage Without a Key, The Gift of Life, The Comeback Kid, Love Leads The Way and *I Love You Perfect,* which co-starred Anthony Denison (*Crime Story, Wiseguy, Undercover*). Her film credits include *Echo Park, First Love, Looker, Skyjacked* and *The Trouble With Dick.*

It seems as though *L.A. Law* has given her the most satisfaction, although she's very clear about one thing: "I'm not going to make *L.A. Law* my life," Dey has emphasized. "I had too much of that pressure from *The Partridge Family.* The new series is just a job."

Adding credence to these words is that fact that season five will be her last one on the show, as Grace Van Owen, like her real-life counterpart, will be seeking out new directions in her life.

CORBIN BERNSEN
(ARNIE BECKER)

One of *L.A. Law's* sleaziest members is Arnie Becker, divorce lawyer extraordinaire, who will sleep with just about any female client, sneak his files from McKenzie-Brackman in the middle of the night to start his own practice, have an affair with his secretary the night before he gets married, then have an affair with a client just several months after he has been wed. All this time, he continues to play martyr, declaring he's being used or victimized. Despite all this, Arnie manages to remain lovable, thanks to Corbin Bernsen's sympathetic portrayal.

"I feel sorry for Arnie Becker," Bernsen, who's married to actress Amanda Pays, recently explained, "because I now know the joys of being with someone you love so much. I know what he's missing and it makes me sad. I've always contended that Becker isn't really just this Marina del Ray mover and shaker with gold chains who says, 'Hey, babe.' He's a single guy looking for answers, the same way I was. (A difference between us is that) Arnie is a playboy. He'll go up to a woman at a party and say, 'Let's go to Spago for dinner.' Me, I'm a hound dog. I'd be standing behind a cactus in the corner.

"For me," he added, "a lot of the wonderful humor in the writing got to come out through the Becker character. The hardest thing about putting this character together was realizing that the guy is a rat, but you don't want the audiences to not like him. Walking that fine line of loving to hate somebody is not easy. Done another way, he might have come off as (someone) you don't care about. At the beginning, he was called a womanizing rat and that was all.

"The thing that might have worried me is that people would get the perception that we have these kind of commedia dell'arte characters, but they aren't really—they are changing. I wanted to say, 'Wait, wait!' But I think that people now have come to know that these characters evolve. Right now I feel Arnie's a guy who's realizing that his system, his modus operandi, doesn't always work. Right now he's in a reevaluation mode.

"I'd like to think that when (Arnie's) manipulating, he's not really sure what he's doing. When you talk about the law, yes, he's the great manipulator, he knows exactly what he's doing. But when it comes to his social life or what he's doing to (his secretary) Roxanne, maybe I don't want to know. Then I would be the villain."

Graduating from UCLA, Bernsen went to New York and appeared in an Off-Off Broadway production of *Lone Star* and a touring company of *Plaza Suite*. He also

spent two years on the soap opera *Ryan's Hope*. His film credits include *S.O.B.*, *King Kong, Eat My Dust, Major League, Bert Rigby, You're a Fool* and *Disorganized Crime*. Recently he starred in Turner Network Television's *Breaking Point* and NBC's *Line of Fire: The Morris Dees Story*.

All indications are that Bernsen will stay with *L.A. Law* throughout the series' entire run. But what of the future?

"I'm afraid to ask," Bernsen has mused. ""But down the road I could see building houses in Montana or Maine and doing community theater. I've gotten my turn. I'd have no complaints."

JILL EIKENBERRY
(ANN KELSEY)

Ann Kelsey is one half of *L.A. Law's* most interesting couples. The character is married to McKenzie-Brackman tax specialist Stuart Markowitz. As we've seen, Ann Kelsey is a tough-as-nails attorney who won't take garbage from anyone. She will seldom compromise her ideals, even when it comes down to the point where she will have to tender her resignation over what she's done. Stuart, on the other hand, is a quiet, schlumpy kind of guy who is Ann's total opposite, devoted to her and the only person who can give her heat and get away with it.

Interestingly, Jill Eikenberry and Michael Tucker, who portray those characters, are married in real life, and each occupy the opposite's position on the show.

"Normally I've played the nice, quiet wife. Kelsey was an interesting, aggressive person who excited me. It's always fun to get the next script and find out whether we're going to like each other in this episode or be angry or have a romantic scene or an argument," Eikenberry told one journalist.

"It's interesting how it affects our lives. We see some big scenes coming up that has an argument in it, and we tend to get a little argumentative at home. If we're working on something romantic, we tend to be romantic. One bedroom scene kept them nervous for a week before filming. We both thought it would have been a lot easier if it had been a stranger we were with. Because then it would have been pretend.

"When I got the part, I was still in New York. So a friend took me to his old, prestigious Wall Street law firm. I met a woman there who'd just been made partner and spent the day with her. She was a litigator. I talked to her about the clothes she wore, about the kind of behavior she had to exhibit in court, about the long hours she kept. It was amazing. Sometimes, when she was in the middle of a big case, she'd spend the night in her office working. Her home life? It was a shambles. She was married, with two children and it was just impossible. [But Ann] is a very interesting part to play.

"Any woman who has a high-powered job in a basically macho profession is faced with a dilemma: how to figure out the right way to be strong. Which is harder for a woman. I don't know why. So I had to create someone who had some anger—who had her hackles up about being manipulated by men in any way. Kelsey doesn't want to reduce Markowitz to a sniveling wimp, but at the same time she's not willing to give over a lot of her strengths. That constant struggle they go through—I think that's really timely. I've had women say to me, 'Now stay strong!' I think

they're afraid I'll go down the path of becoming the nice-lady-behind-the-man, the way so many women characters have. But I really don't think (the writers are) inclined to go that way, so I'm not worried."

After attending Yale University, Eikenberry appeared on the short-lived play *Moonchildren,* and was featured a year later Off-Broadway in *Beggars Opera.* Other stage roles include *All Over Town* (directed by Dustin Hoffman), *Summer Brave, Uncommon Woman, The Eccentricities of a Nightingale, Watch on the Rhine, Onward Victoria.* She has appeared in such films as *Rich Kids, Butch and Sundance: The Early Days, Hide in Plain Sight* and *Arthur.*

Television has featured her in *My Boyfriend's Back, Yes to You: The Diane Martin Story, Family Sins, Assault and Matrimony, A Stoning in Fulham County* and *Archie's Wife.*

Eikenberry and Tucker have expressed their interest in remaining with the series for some time to come.

ALAN RACHINS
(DOUGLAS BRACKMAN, JR.)

One of *L.A. Law's* sleaziest characters is undoubtedly Douglas Brackman, Jr., office manager at McKenzie-Brackman, and generally considered, in his own words, to be the office son of a bitch. All that concerns Brackman is the bottom line, and he is completely insensitive to the needs of those around him. Proof of this came in an early episode where he mentioned that senior partner and founding member Leland McKenzie had hardly clocked any billable hours and therefore wasn't entitled to a full partner's share. Needless to say, McKenzie put him right in his place.

In the years that followed, audiences witnessed a gradual softening of Brackman's character, making him somewhat more likeable and sympathetic. This has come through Brackman's divorce from wife Sheila (played by Rachins' real life spouse Joanna Frank), his temporary position as a Small Claim's Court judge, a reunion with two step-brothers he never knew he had (who turned out to be sleazier than Douglas ever could), problems with his ability to have sexual relations and several dates with *Wheel of Fortune's* Vanna White. After all this time, Brackman's not such a bad guy after all. Interestingly, Alan Rachins finds some emotional similarities between he and his on-screen persona.

"Douglas has been under his father's domination," he's said. "He never got a chance to really find out who he is himself. His father had the law firm and said, 'You'll go into the law firm.' He feels a lot of pressure about living up to his father's image as a major lawyer. Had I gone into my father's business and not broken away, Douglas and I would have had a lot in common. He's not as good a lawyer as his father. But he might have been much happier and a nicer guy if he had done other things. (Thanks to Douglas) I dress better. I also look out for my own interests better. On the other hand, I worry more about acting belligerent. If I get annoyed at the post office, I'm afraid people will say, 'He's just like Douglas.'"

About the series, he's added, "This show is about having it all. But it goes further—deals with a more important issue: What is it like when you get there?"

Rachins' stage roles include such shows as *After the Rain, Madrian the Seventh, The Trojan Women, Oh! Calcutta* and *La Cage Aux Folles.*

His television credits include *Hill Street Blues, Fall Guy, Hart to Hart, Knight Rider, Quincy, Paris,* the television movies *Single Women, Married Men* and *Perry Mason and The Case of the Silent Stranger.*

MICHELE GREENE
(ABBY PERKINS)

Like the rest of the ensemble, Abby Perkins has gone through quite a metamorphosis over the last five years. When we are first introduced to her, Abby is a law associate at McKenzie-Brackman, doing little more than follow-up work, looking kind of plain and ordinary and dealing with an alcoholic husband who regularly beats her and then kidnaps their son when a court-issued restraining order keeps him away. Essentially, Abby is everyone's punching bag.

Things changed, however, as Abby started asserting herself and improving everything about her. On the surface, she suddenly became a knock-out and very fashionable. Professionally she moved forward as a lawyer, quitting the firm when associate Victor Sifuentes got a hefty raise and she didn't, opening up her own practice and then, having impressed Leland McKenzie so much, being invited to work at the firm once again. Subsequently, she became a great lawyer, though in season five it's a question of whether or not she will remain, as Victor has become a partner and she hasn't. That will undoubtedly be decided by the writers.

"There was a definite choice on the part of the producer to have this girl be really unhip," Greene has detailed in the past. "(Terry Louise Fisher) said, 'Abigail's like a woman who would have taken a wagon train west. She might have hated it, but she would have made it.' So next to certain lines in my script I write, 'Pioneer Ab.' They wanted me to look sort of drab. They wanted the character to start out not having a real sense of herself, except that she was smart and had gone to law school.

"Abby is such a struggling character. She's been the office mole, stuck in the library researching statutes. She doesn't have much confidence in herself. But that's only part of her problem. The partners (didn't have) any confidence in her, either. I meet lawyers my age all the time. They tell me that after leaving law school excited that they're going to be trying cases and making a difference, they find themselves working in the back room—with no personal life at all.

"We don't do any yelling on this show. I got the part mostly because Steven (Bochco) had cast me as a baseball wife in his previous series, *Bay City Blues,* which was not a big hit show. So I went along with the part of Abby in *L.A. Law* but I hated it. At the end of the first year I said, 'Look. I guess every show has to have the obligatory female victim in it, but I don't want to spend all my time crying on camera.' The guys looked at me and Steve said, 'You're right. But it'll take time.'

"He's a feminist at heart, and I guess I touched a raw nerve. I spent two seasons saying, 'I'm doing the research on the such-and-such case,' or 'Hey, Ann, wanna grab a cup of coffee?' Benny, the retarded office boy, had more challenging scenes. But they wrote me out of my corner. Abby left the firm. Got a better haircut. Then she got tough."

While attending USC, Greene managed to land roles on such television series as *Eight is Enough, Laverne and Shirley, Highway to Heaven* and *Simon and Simon.* Upon graduation, she became a series regular on the aforementioned *Bay City Blues* and has been featured in the TV movies *Going to the Chapel, Double Standard, Seduced* and *Perry Mason Returns.* Her stage credits include *Dames at Sea, Once Upon a Mattress, Electra, The Shadow Box, Tales From the Vienna Woods* and *The Suicide.*

Despite any minor complaints she might have, Greene emphasizes to the press that she is happy where she is, though she remains a tiny bit paranoid that it could all be over in a flash.

"I'd been trained not to get my hopes up," she said. "Even after *L.A. Law* was a hit, I wouldn't relax. I was the last one to decorate my dressing room. Susan (Dey) or Corbin (Bernsen) would pass by and say, 'Michele, *please* get a plant!' It could end next week—Abby could get hit by a car—but I certainly hope not. It feels so good."

JIMMY SMITS
(VICTOR SIFUENTES)

"I'm always hearing from single women that their dates are so weird. So I switched the sex."

—Terry Louise Fisher, Supervising Producer re: Victor Sifuentes

Victor Sifuentes is perhaps one of the best lawyers that McKenzie-Brackman has. In the hands of actor Jimmy Smits, he is a man of class and determination who busts his butt to get the job done. This is not to say that other members of the crew aren't as effective, but Sifuentes can argue a point without making himself look like a bad guy. You sense that when he puts someone on the stand, someone innocent, he truly regrets having to put them through any additional anguish. If you're guilty, he'll get you on the stand in such a way that it won't even look like an attack, therefore you'll get no sympathy from the jury.

Sifuentes began his career as far as television viewers are concerned in the Public Defender's office, and was brought in to McKenzie-Brackman because of his abilities in the courtroom. Over the past half a decade, we have seen him master his skills to become the highly efficient lawyer discussed above. The one recurring problem in Sifuentes' life is the odd assortment of women he has been involved with over the years, one more crazy than the next. The one exception was Allison Gottlieb, who was eventually raped by someone else and had to go away because Victor reminded her of the whole incident. It seems like Sifuentes just can't get a break. Come on, guys!

"We're alike in that Victor has gone to college and he's involved in a profession he's very good at," explained Smits. "Certainly that's not something that's being explored a lot on television. The characters are fallible, people with dark sides to them. (The show's popularity was surprising.) We knew we were putting out wonderful work, but it isn't the average TV fare that people are used to. When I read the pilot, I knew it was a heavy-duty show. I loved the double meanings, the adult humor, the fact that it wasn't bang-bang, shoot 'em up. The characters weren't all good or all bad, and there was a little edge to everything.

"It's not very Hollywoodish here. Jokes are everywhere. We go to see dailies together during lunch. There's a lot of goofing around with the crew. I love the fact that everybody's head is screwed on straight, that no one is fighting over whose trailer is best. This show is pretty special."

Jimmy Smits has appeared on stage in Joseph Papp's production of *Hamlet* and

Ballad of Soapy Smith. In addition to co-starring in the pilot for *Miami Vice* and such television films as *Dangerous Affection* and *Glitz,* his screen credits include *Running Scared, The Believers, Vital Signs, Old Gringo* and the forthcoming *Fires Within*.

Smits, who won the 1990 Emmy Award for best actor in a dramatic television series, has indicated that the fifth season of *L.A. Law* might be his last, as he wants to pursue a career in motion pictures. If true, this will be a major loss to the series.

MICHAEL TUCKER
(STUART MARKOWITZ)

Lovable tax attorney Stuart Markowitz remains one of the most cuddly of all the *L.A. Law* regulars. He basically has remained a good-natured man who is somewhat more incorruptible than his associates. He is devoted entirely to his wife, Ann Kelsey, and their son, Matthew. Over the years he has developed into a fine lawyer, handling some of the smaller cases the firm has had to deal with. In season five, he suffered a heart attack and this unleashed a group of demons that caused him to move away from his wife for a time until he worked it all out. Needless to say, he did.

As stated in the Jill Eikenberry bio, she and Tucker, who are married in real life, are actually the opposite of the characters they play.

"The biggest problem with committing to do a television series is that many television characters are two-dimensional," said Tucker. "That really locks you into a very narrow person. But these characters clearly are 360-degree people. I feel that they could be put in any situation and behave as human beings. A good writer and producer understands that if you write too close to a person it will be harder for the person to play the role. Ann Kelsey is the opposite of Jill. She's much more strident and aggressive. If Steve had cast a strident, aggressive actress, Ann Kelsey would have lost a full range of emotions that she now has.

"Many husbands and wives won't work together," he explained, pointing to the fact that they appeared in an episode of *Hill Street Blues* together. "They have arguments, their egos clash, they get very upset with each other. But Jill and I had a good time, and I think the idea of our working together on *L.A. Law* came out of our experience on *Hill Street*."

Tucker was graduated from Carnegie Tech and appeared on stage in *Moonchildren, Arturo Ui, Waiting For Godot, Modligliani, The Rivals, Mother Courage, Oh What a Lovely War, The Merry Wives of Windsor, Shakespeare in the Park, Comedy of Errors* and *Trelawney of the Wells*. TV movies include *The Quinns, Vampire* and *A Night Full of Rain*. Big screen productions are *An Unmarried Woman, The Eyes of Laura Mars, The Goodbye People, Diner, The Purple Rose of Cairo, Diner* and *Radio Days*.

He and Jill Eikenberry plan on staying with *L.A. Law* for some time to come.

SUSAN RUTTAN
(ROXANNE MELMAN)

*I*f Arnie Becker has been given any saving grace on this planet, it is his secretary, Roxanne Melman. No matter what he gets himself involved in, Roxanne is there to lend an emotional hand or support in any way that she can. Although in love with Arnie during the first couple of seasons of the show, the two of them never consummated their relationship, fearful that it would destroy their friendship.

At the beginning, if you were to look up the word "chump" in a dictionary, Roxanne's picture would appear. Arnie used their friendship constantly, and when it came time to get a raise he held back and she threatened to quit. Ultimately he gave in, and that's when she began to change. As the series has continued, Rox has grown into an independent woman, having faced personal bankruptcy, marriage to a man she didn't love (who knew this little fact before they said "I do") and divorce (which made her a fairly wealthy woman).

She has learned how to better assert herself and deal with people. It's been a constant growth process for her, and this basic whiner has become a full-bodied person.

As is true in most situations, Roxanne is the secretary that her boss could not live without. Arnie would be lost if she were to leave him.

"When we were shooting the pilot," Ruttan reflected, "the director called each of the actors by name. Except for me. When he wanted me, he said, 'Get the secretary.' (I had worked as a secretary) so I know what it means to be making less money than almost everybody else around. (Now) Roxanne is in the process of becoming liberated. But no matter what changes she goes through, there is still that expectation that someday Arnie will look at her and say, 'You are the one I've been looking for all my life.' She has a blind spot with regard to this man. She's human.

"I (also) think people are relieved that it's not Joan Collins playing Roxanne. This character is not climbing over bodies to get where she wants. She's a person trying to grow up and find her way in this world. It's hard. I sympathize."

On television, Ruttan has had roles in *The Misadventures of Sheriff Lobo, Quincy, Remington Steele, Bosom Buddies, Newhart, Night Court, Buffalo Bill, Second Sight, By Reason of Insanity, Do You Remember Love?, Scorned and Swindled, Bay Coven, Take My Daughters, Please, Fire and Rain* and *Sweet Fifteen*. Films include *Growing Pains, Honky Tonk Freeway, Independence Day, Changes Are* and *Bad Dreams*.

In Ruttan's hands, Roxanne Melman will continue to discover what her life is all about, and the directions she must travel.

BLAIR UNDERWOOD
(JONATHAN ROLLINS)

*T*he law associates of McKenzie-Brackman have played an integral role in the development of the series. Next to Victor Sifuentes, none has had quite the impact Jonathan Rollins has.

Full of confidence from the moment he was interviewed for the job, Rollins has been like a steamroller, not allowing anything to get in his way—or believing that it could. While far from ruthless, he is able to achieve a great deal simply from his cockiness. There often have been instances where his ego has been to his detriment, but he has learned from every mistake and, through the course of the series, he has become one of the firm's best lawyers. As Stuart Markowitz noted, "He's the kind of lawyer that people hire. He's the kind of lawyer that makes money."

In seasons four and five, in particular, Rollins has truly developed into an individual who must be seen to be believed. For evidence, check out the season four episode in which he is unable to reveal the location of a dead body to the boy's parents because it would betray attorney-client privilege, or the opening few episodes of season five in which he embroiled in a race-related murder trial. Aside from a character standpoint, Underwood's acting skills have developed as well.

"I think people would like to know why (Jonathan) is so relentless about proving himself all the time," Underwood's mused. "While Rollins is determined to succeed in no uncertain terms, we are certain to see more of his personal side as time goes by and his sexual side as well. In some ways I have a lot of admiration for the way he handles himself. But he thinks he can do whatever he wants. Regardless of who tells him what to do and how to do it, he's got a better way. So far he's gotten results, but he's got to learn it's a team effort."

Following educational pursuits at Carnegie-Mellon, Underwood managed to make an appearance on *The Cosby Show* and then landed a three month stint on *One Life to Live*. From there he co-starred in the short-lived series *Downtown*, in the motion picture *Krush Groove,* Turner Network Television's *Heat Wave* (which co-starred James Earl Jones and Cicely Tyson) and in the critically acclaimed NBC movie, *Murder in Mississippi.*

For now, he's satisfied that *L.A. Law* is having such an impact on its audience.

"I was in Atlanta recently," he said, "when this woman shared her gratitude with me for providing a positive role model for her son, who is now determined to be a lawyer. I consider myself extremely fortunate that I've been able to express myself in a quality project such as *L.A. Law* that is both critically acclaimed and appreciat-

ed by the public."

At the moment, Underwood seems to be keeping his attention on his adventures as Jonathan Rollins

LARRY DRAKE
(BENNY STULWICZ)

Benny Stulwicz is perhaps one of the most surprising additions to *L.A. Law*. This retarded man first appeared on the show when he was arrested for robbery, but was later cleared by the judge for the simple reason that he clearly did not know he was doing something illegal. He returned in a subsequent episode in which his mother, knowing that she will be dying soon, asks Abby Perkins what can be done with Benny and Abby offers to get him a job there as a messenger.

So effective was Benny in his job that the firm decided to keep him on, and so strong a presence was actor Larry Drake—who is *not* retarded—that the critics lauded the positive image of the retarded that the show projected. Benny became a regular, his role constantly enlarging.

Drake prepared for the role by visiting with a retarded man named Jeff Miller. "Jeff reminds me of something in me that I can put into Benny," the actor related to *People* magazine. "When Jeff gets nervous he stutters, but as Benny I'll go more to a searching-for-the-word type thing, with a lot of 'ums' and 'wells.' I let my whole face go because it pulls my eyes down a little. My eyes tend to cross anyway, so I let them drift, which puts a strange cast on them."

Drake has appeared on stage in *The Stick Wife, Greater Tuna, Of Mice and Men, Kiss Me, Kate, Arsenic and Old Lace, Henry IV-Part I, Terre Nova, Richard II, Richard III, St. Joan, A Texas Trilogy, The Learned Ladies, Jumpers, The Merry Wives of Windsor, The Lion in Winter, Oklahoma, The Rainmaker, Man of La Mancha, Harvey, Cactus Flower, Fiddler on the Roof, The Fantastiks* and *The Silver Whistle*.

On television he has been featured in *Too Good to Be True, Dark Night of the Scarecrow, Werewolf, Hunter, Dalton* and *Hardcastle and McCormick*. His film credits are *The Karate Kid, The Big Brawl* and *The White Lions*. In an attempt to go against the potential typecasting of Benny, Drake starred as a psychotic Santa Claus in an episode of HBO's *Tales From the Crypt* and as the villain in Universal's highly successful, *Darkman*.

"I don't know if I'm a star now," he said, "or just a little meteor that may burn out soon. I've done fine in this business, but I've never made quite enough money to have a family or have many options. I keep looking at my life and thinking, 'If I'm going to get out of this business, I'd better do it soon.' I don't know how long it'll last. It could be my 15 minutes of fame."

RICHARD DYSART
(LELAND MCKENZIE)

Overseeing all of McKenzie-Brackman is Leland McKenzie himself.

For the first few season, McKenzie was the perfect father figure for his employees, offering advice when necessary and always being there with a kind word or a strong reprimand when necessary. In fact, Leland was such an image of perfection that real-life alter ego Richard Dysart told the producers, "Jesus Christ, knock me off this . . . horse!"

Steven Bochco and the other writer/producers apparently listened. In season four we saw everything taking its toll on Leland. The in-house battles were becoming more intense, clients were being lost, revenues were down and he just didn't have the strength to do it all any more, so he backed away. Eventually he did have to step forward again, and when he did so he was stronger than ever, although he had picked up some negative tendencies in terms of the decisions he made. While no longer perfect, Leland had definitely become human.

Dysart's stage performances include *Our Town, All in Good Time, That Championship Season, The Little Foxes, Another Part of the Forest* and *Black Angel*. On television he has starred in *The Last Days of Patton, Blood and Orchids, Malice in Wonderland, The Autobiography of Miss Jane Pittman, Bitter Harvest, Sandburg's Lincoln, First You Cry, Last Days of Patton* and as Harry Truman in both *War and Remembrance* and *Day One*.

Motion picture credits are *The Hospital, The Falcon and the Snowman, Day of the Locust, Pale Rider, Being There, Wall Street* and *Back to the Future Part III*.

Of *L.A. Law* Dysart has said, "Steven Bochco, David Kelley and Bill Finkelstein have provided us with strong scripts and diverse, interesting characters. The true stars of the series are the *scripts*— and what a blessing that is for the television viewer."

THE EPISODES

The ensemble cast of LA LAW interact in varied and complex ways with some action beginning in one episode only to be pursued in a later one. The events of one storyline often effect those of another. Forewith is a complex guide through the labyrinth that has been LA LAW.

Jill Eikenberry and Michael Tucker (husband and wife off-screen) portray married partners in the law firm of McKenzie, Brackman, Chaney, Kusak & Becker.

SEASON ONE

PRODUCTION STAFF
Executive Producer: Steven Bochco
Co-Executive Producer: Gregory Hoblit
Supervising Producer: Terry Louise Fisher
Producer: Ellen S. Pressman
Producer: Scott Goldstein
Coordinating Producer: Phillip Goldfarb

REGULAR CAST
Harry Hamlin: Michael Kuzak
Jill Eikenberry: Ann Kelsey
Michele Greene: Abby Perkins
Alan Rachins: Douglas Brackman, Jr.
Jimmy Smits: Victor Sifuentes
Michael Tucker: Stuart Markowitz
Richard Dysart: Leland McKenzie
Corbin Bernsen: Arnold Becker
Susan Ruttan: Roxanne Melman
Susan Dey: Grace Van Owen

Episode One

"L.A. Law"

Directed by Gregory Hoblit

Guest Stars: Juanin Clay (Alice Ratakowsky), Patrick Cronin (Lester Mestman)

Our introduction to the law firm of McKenzie, Brackman, Chaney and Kuzak is certainly an auspicious one, with the audience getting quick looks at members of the ensemble.

Arnie Becker arrives at the office, where he is greeted by secretary Roxanne Melman. She starts over his schedule for the day. No sooner does he sit at his desk than a desperate man named Rick Hobart enters the office, pointing a gun. It seems Becker was the lawyer who worked out the man's ex-wife's divorce settlement, destroying him financially. Fortunately for Becker, the gun is loaded with blanks.

Meanwhile, Roxanne finds Norman Chaney, the firm's senior partner, with his head against the desk, his face half buried in a plate of food, dead of an apparent heart attack. The news is crushing to Senior Partner Leland McKenzie. Before he can grieve, he receives an important phone call from client John Pregerson. He wants the firm to handle the case of his son, who has been arrested.

Douglas Brackman interviews Georgia Buckner as a potential secretary and associate Andrew Taylor and clerk Bruce Pollack find her attractive. Elsewhere, Roxanne is talking to Ann Kelsey about being the one who found Chaney's body.

At police headquarters in Hollywood, partner Michael Kuzak intervenes in a near fistfight between public defender Victor Sifuentes and Sergeant McKoskey over one of Sifuentes' clients. He then meets with Detective Lester to discuss his client, Justin Pregerson,

charged with raping a woman dying of leukemia. This meeting leads to one with the client himself, who defends his action by saying that the victim was asking for it.

At a staff meeting, the first big issue on Becker's mind is who will get Chaney's office. Everyone, particularly McKenzie, jumps on him for his insensitivity. As the meeting breaks up, associate Abby Perkins is met by her husband, Jim, who is drunk and wants to borrow money.

Becker then discusses a divorce settlement with client Celia Robinson, pointing out that her husband has been unfaithful on numerous occasions. He tells her to go for a larger settlement.

The following day, as Kuzak awaits the arraignment of Pregerson, a fellow lawyer suggests he consider Sifuentes as an associate in the firm. After the arraignment, Kuzak meets with counsel for two other members of the group accused of raping Michelle Moore. The lawyers, much to Kuzak's revulsion, detail their plans to keep things going until the victim either quits or dies.

Ann Kelsey and Perkins meet with Lester Mestman, representative of an insurance company refusing to pay for a CAT scan for client Celia Robinson.

At the courthouse, Michelle Moore is put on the stand and lawyers for the defendants turn things around so that it seems she is the one who is at fault. Things go from bad to worse when Moore says what she would really like to do is get a gun and kill the three men who raped her. Judge Ratakowski holds her in contempt and has her taken to a holding cell. When Kuzak protests, he, too, is found in contempt and, due to a large number of unpaid traffic tickets, is arrested.

He is put in the cell next to Moore. She tells him her treatment in court has convinced her not to proceed with the case. Kuzak counters that if she did get a gun to do the men in, he wouldn't lose any sleep. Moore replies, "That's the difference between us. I would."

Kuzak's later attempt to get McKenzie to take him off the case falls on deaf ears.

Back at the firm, detective Angela Sipriano brings Becker photographic evidence of Lydia Graham's husband in the midst of one of his many affairs.

At memorial services for Norman Chaney, McKenzie leads off the eulogies, followed by Stuart Markowitz. Everyone is stunned when Brackman's secretary, Georgia, stands at the podium and announces she had a sex change operation and that she and Chaney had been lovers.

Dr. Mandel examines Celia Robinson and says she might have had a better chance of recovery from her brain tumor had it been diagnosed earlier, but because the insurance company wouldn't pay for it, she couldn't. As a result, Kelsey sets out on her new task of proving the insurance company operated in bad faith in its dealings with her.

In the courtroom, Moore is back on the stand and feigns memory loss, attributed to the medication she is taking. The judge dismisses the case, as there is not sufficient evidence to support it. Justin Pregerson is still nervous, noting Moore's earlier threat to kill him. He is unable to gain a sympathetic ear.

Having seen Sifuentes in action, Kuzak is impressed enough to ask Victor to lunch with him, Brackman and McKenzie. Sifuentes is not impressed, believing they want him to do nothing more than handle the cases no one else is interested in. Insulted, he leaves.

Lester Mestman's extremely small settlement offer to Kelsey and Perkins is rejected.

Becker, unbeknownst to his client, introduces the photographic proof of

George Graham in an amorous embrace. Lydia hates Becker for doing this. He tells her someday she will thank him for it, as it helped get her life on a straight path again, thanks to the improved settlement.

High on cocaine, Pregerson nears Kuzak in the underground garage, asking for money, as his father has cut him off. Kuzak refuses. Justin pulls out a gun and robs him. At a nearby bar, Kuzak sits with a police officer he knows, implies the robbery just took place and leaves. Eventually, Pregerson is arrested again, this time on a new string of charges.

Kuzak recommends he plead guilty to the rape, so the other charges can be dropped. He considers this and quickly agrees. He and his two cohorts are sentenced to 18 months in prison—a small victory, but a victory nonetheless.

At a party ending the episode, a somewhat inebriated Kelsey asks Markowitz to sleep with her, Perkins is splashed in the face by her husband's drink, Brackman is served with a sex discrimination suit filed by Georgia, and Victor Sifuentes agrees to join the firm on a trial basis.

(NOTE: As he did on Hill Street Blues, *Steven Bochco brings gritty reality and an incredibly strong ensemble cast. There is not a weak performance among the regulars, and the viewer can only anticipate the stories yet to come. By electing to focus on the professional as well as personal lives of his protagonists, Bochco has revolutionized television's portrayal of lawyers. Move over, Perry Mason!)*

Episode Two

"Those Lips, That Eye"

Directed by Gregory Hoblit

Guest Stars: Sarah Abrell (Lisa), Tony Soper (Bruce Pollack), Rob Knepper

(Georgia Buckner), Mario Van Peebles (Taylor), Boyd Gaines (Jim Perkins), Patrick Cronin (Lester Mestman), Ellen Blake (Elizabeth Brand), Patricia Huston (Hilda Brunscheiger), Vanda Berra (Helen Shuster), Robert MacKenzie (Modell), Paco Vela (Arturo Figueroa), Loyda Ramos (Isabel Figueroa), Tanya Russel (Mary), Robert Alan Browne (Judge Satren), CCH Pounder (Judge Robin), Maggie Han (Sandy), Ellen Gerstein (Bailiff), Kyle Scott Jackson (Bailiff), Charles Walker (Security Guard), Jason Corbett (Gallagher)

As Kuzak and Sifuentes watch another attorney, Sy Modell, succeed in clearing millionaire client Nelson Gallagher of a murder charge, Kuzak catches sight of Deputy District Attorney Grace Van Owen and is *very* impressed. Later, in the corridor, the victim's father, Arturo Figueroa, pulls a gun and threatens to kill Gallagher. Sifuentes talks the man out of committing a murder himself. He offers to defend Figueroa on the charges which undoubtedly will be filed.

Following their night of passion, Markowitz tries everything he can to get the attention of Kelsey, but to no avail. She claims she's too busy with the Celia Robinson case to have a social life. Brackman eventually voices his feeling that Kelsey and Perkins should settle the case out of court, which infuriates them.

At the staff meeting, Andrew Taylor is beside himself over the hiring of Sifuentes. All it means to him is that the pecking order might change, making it that much tougher for him to someday make partner. He declares he no will no longer be the firm's "company nigger," to which McKenzie responds: "I wouldn't tolerate that kind of talk about you, sir. I certainly won't tolerate it from you either."

Taylor warns Sifuentes he'll be given

all the garbage cases so the rest of the partners won't have to soil their hands. With that he leaves. Moments later, McKenzie asks him to reconsider—which he refuses—and offers to write him a glowing reference letter.

Elsewhere in the office, Mestman brings in a new, but still low, settlement offer in the Robinson case. Kelsey says the settlement will be $1 million, payable at the end of business that day, or the price goes up to $1.2 million. He comes in the next day with a check for $1 million, but because he's late, she demands the higher price. Threatening that they'll see each other in court, he leaves. When McKenzie hears what happened, he is furious, saying Kelsey let her ego get in the way of a good settlement for both her client and the firm.

Becker has agreed to be Perkins' lawyer in her divorce suit. She now has a black eye and is escorted to court by him. Her husband, completely drunk, also is brought in. Judge Robin tells him he has one week to sober up and hire an attorney before she meets with them.

At the next staff meeting, Brackman comes in with a check from Mestman for $1,200,000. McKenzie congratulates Kelsey and she admits he was right—she did indeed allow her own ego to get in the way of her job. She declares she will not allow it to happen again. Success ringing in her ears, Kelsey finally agrees to go to dinner with a delighted Markowitz.

At the courthouse, Sifuentes tells Kuzak he managed to get all charges dropped against Arturo, so the man will not be jailed. Van Owen, who Kuzak has taken out for dinner, comes up to him and says she can no longer date him. A few moments later, the trio hears word that Arturo shot and killed Nelson Gallagher . They go out for drinks to let this sink in. Sifuentes, in particular, is sickened by the events.

(A storyline like the one involving Arturo is quite different than anything we would have expected from a television series as the form in most cases almost always requires an uplifting ending. Here we are given a father's rage unleashed when the system doesn't work. It's not treated as a Death Wish-*like comic book fantasy, but with gritty reality.)*

As the night ends, Van Owen drives Kuzak home and tells him the reason she can't see him anymore is that she's engaged. Kuzak argues that they definitely feel something for each other, but she counters that it's not enough for her to break off the engagement.

(NOTE: Mario Van Peebles (Andrew Taylor) has gone on to quite a successful television directing career. He also stars in the series Sonny Spoon *and such films as* Jaws–The Revenge. *Character actor Robert Alan Browne (Judge Satren) is probably best known to horror fans as diner owner Mr. Statler in* Psycho II *and* Psycho III.*)*

Episode Three

"The House of the Rising Flan"

Directed by E.W. Swackhamer

Guest Stars: Kenny D'Aquilla (Suit), Michael Horton (Tom Locklin), Joanna Frank (Sheila Brackman), Roy Brocksmith (Marv Fletcher), Ellen Blake (Elizabeth), Bill Macy (Irving Lewis), Bel Sandre (Estella Escobar), David Wohl (Walter Resler), Felton Perry (Tuttle), Sandra J. Marshall (Marjorie Locklin), Patricia Huston (Hilda Brunscheiger), Aki Aleong (Judge Nozaki), Ezekiel Moss (Lafolette), Kathy Spritz (Teacher), Patrick Stehr (Jamie), Catherine Keener (Waitress), Cec Verrell (Angela Sipriano), Judy Landers (Dinitra Lewis), Mary Gregory (Judge Pendelton)

Having accepted a dinner invitation to the Brackman's, Sifuentes is mortified and insulted to learn that the only reason they invited him was to meet their housekeeper. They hope he will find her attractive and interesting enough to marry—even though it would be a sham marriage—so she can stay in the country and they won't lose her. Furious at their obvious racist attitude, Victor tells Brackman off and leaves.

In court, Kuzak is representing young Jamie Locklin, supposedly injured for life in an accident at an amusement park. He is confronted with the statement that Jamie actually was adopted by the Locklins and his name legally changed to protect the fact that he had been injured years earlier.

Meanwhile, Markowitz and millionaire Irving Lewis, who has brought with him a tape of his "actress" wife Dinitra, singing and dancing in a completely erotic and explicit manner, are attempting an IRS appeal. They meet with IRS representative Marv Fletcher, who disallows Irving's tax deductions because his wife is not really an actress in the truest sense of the word. Markowitz tries countering with a variety of fabricated precedent-setting cases. Fletcher leaves to consider this, and Markowitz is racked with guilt for having told such lies. Irving warns him not to tell the IRS the truth, or the firm will be fired.

Next day, Fletcher agrees that if the man pays off his back taxes, he will not be charged any penalties. Irving still isn't happy, particularly after he is told what he owes. He eventually decides to pay when he learns his wife left him for her partner on the video tape.

Abbey goes to pick up her son, Eric, at nursery school, and learns the boy's father had picked him up some time earlier. Getting Becker to go with her, they head for police headquarters to file a kidnapping charge, as an order was issued restraining him from contacting Abby and Eric.

In court, Jamie's father takes the stand and comes across as completely sympathetic. Despite what the evidence may indicate to the contrary, the amusement company fears losing the case. The company's lawyer, Walter Resler, tries to settle out of court. Kuzak recommends that the Locklins accept the offer as it is possible they will face charges of fraud if the "family history" is checked out any further. They accept. Kuzak later tries once again to get things going with Van Owen, but with no success.

Detective Sipriano tells Abby of her husband and child's last known whereabouts, but doesn't hold out high hopes that they will be able to find them.

(NOTE: Character actor Bill Macy (Irving Lewis) co-starred with Bea Arthur in the Norman Lear TV series, Maude. *Judy Landers (Dinitra Lewis) has been in numerous films and television series, usually as an air-head sexpot.)*

Episode Four

"The Princess and the Wiener King"

Directed by E.W. Swackhamer

Guest Stars: Patricia Huston (Hilda Brunscheiger), Christian Clemenson (Pommerantz), Maggie Han (Sandy), Anne Haney (Judge Travelini), Dean Devlin (Christopher Sullivan), Jill Johnson (Young Woman), Shannon Sullivan (Professor), Ellen Blake (Elizabeth), Mark Schilder (Preppy), Murray Rubin (Manager), Louis Ellias (Guy at bar), Joe Costanza (Bartender), Richard Gates (Kevin Crenshaw), David Andrews (Mr. Simmons), Carol Potter (Mrs. Simmons), Matthew Faison (Reading), Pierrette Grace (Tracey Simmons), Adam Arkin (Richard Kendall), Cynthia Harris (Iris), Paul Ben-Victor (Costellano), Abel Franco (Judge Rivera), Roma Alvarez (Mrs. Rosario), Alicia Esparga (Senora), Bill Macy (Irving Lewis), Judy Landers (Dinitra Lewis)

While McKenzie is appalled at the economic concerns of students to whom he is guest lecturing, Brackman is meeting with dozens of Hispanic women who have come to the office wanting to be hired as his new housekeeper. The outer offices of McKenzie-Brackman are filled with them.

Meanwhile, Irv Lewis has gotten together with Arnie Becker and Markowitz to lay down the groundwork for his divorce from Dinitra. Markowitz advances the notion that his wife will undoubtedly owe him a great deal of money in back taxes. They eventually meet with Dinitra Lewis and Reading, her lawyer, and tell her about the back taxes she owes Irving. Surprisingly, she agrees to pay anything she has to in order to get out of the marriage. The plain truth is that she just isn't happy. Irving is furious about this turn of events, and Becker offers to take him to the strip joint that the woman is currently working in. Irving and she get together, talk things out and part as friends, Irving's venom having worked itself out.

One of McKenzie's students, Jeffrey Sullivan, comes to the office and praises the words that the senior partner spoke, emphasizing that he concurs with the man's assessment that pro bono cases are extremely important. McKenzie is so taken with the young man's enthusiasm that he hires him as a law clerk. Iris, McKenzie's secretary, calls Sullivan's praise nothing more than brownnosing, and doesn't trust him. As the daily routine is disrupted somewhat by Jeffrey, she goes to McKenzie about it, but he claims that *she* is the one who has a problem.

Abby is having problems of her own. So concerned is she over Eric's disappearance that her work is beginning to suffer. Ann Kelsey is the only one who sympathizes with her. Unfortunately, Abby can't afford the time off.

At roughly the same time, Kelsey and Markowitz' relationship is getting strong. When he brings her to his house, she realizes he is rich.

Courthouse: Sifuentes represents a 13-year-old girl named Tracey Simmons, who murdered her older brother after he attempted to rape her. On the side, opposing counsel suggests to Sifuentes that Tracey might be better off in Juvenile Hall rather than in the home where all this occurred. Sifuentes comes to the conclusion that Tracey's father may have molested her sexually as well, and that history has a good chance of repeating itself. Sifuentes goes to Mrs. Simmons and does his best to get her to file charges against her husband before they have another tragedy on' their hands. Ultimately she does.

Kuzak continues to pursue Grace Van Owen with little luck. To get to understand his "competition" better, he invites her fiance, Kevin Crenshaw, to lunch under the pretense that the Trial Lawyer's Association is planning to conduct an evaluation of Van Owen. Before the conversation can continue, Grace shows up and is shocked to see them together. Later, she lashes into Kuzak for having the nerve to do what he did, but that night she comes by his apartment and apologizes for her outburst. They share a kiss, resulting in a somewhat frightened Van Owen fleeing from the apartment.

(NOTE: It is a tribute to the talents of Harry Hamlin and Susan Dey that they are so able to create a sense of sexual electricity between their characters of Kuzak and Van Owen.)

Episode Five

"Simian Changed Evening"

Directed by E.W. Swackhamer

Karen Austin (Hillary Mishkin), Bob Tzudiker (Gordon Stern), Bill Marcus (Judge Schroeder), George Coe (Judge Vance), Richard Gates (Kevin Crenshaw), Dennis Robertson (Carlton Gertz), Don Sparks (Russell Spitzer), Harold Gould (Harry Finneman), John H. Fields (Anthony Cavelli), Patricia Huston (Hilda), Lance Rosen (Jeffrey Rykman), Terry Burns (Ralph Eastman), Dale Raoul (Dr. Penrod), Eugene Williams (Leon), Sharon Rosen (Witch), Lorinne Vozoff (Margaret Finneman), Dorothy Dells (Mrs. Stuzicki), Chip Lucia (Mitchen Mishkin), Michael Griswold (Judge Connelly), Kurt Fuller (Clifford Gild), Ernie Orsatti (Stunt), Randolph Pitkin (Gorilla), Jim Habif (Mr. Stuzicki)

Arnie Becker expresses interest in taking on some entertainment law cases. McKenzie is very much opposed, fearing the kind of clients such an effort would bring in. Becker nonetheless proceeds with the case of Hillary Mishkin, half of a writer/director team which is breaking up. It's obvious that the two are attracted to each other, but they refrain from sleeping together—at least for a little while. The first thing Becker does is evaluate the two projects the couple developed. He suggests Hillary keep the art film and let her husband take the science fiction epic. Both parties accept this and Hillary definitely proves to be the more prudent of the two. She and Arnie end up sleeping together.

Kuzak is handling a case in which Harry Finneman is attempting to get the right to have himself stuffed once he dies so that he can remain at the home that he helped build over the decades. He also wants to be near his wife for the rest of her life. Various people are brought in to discuss the moral and health pros and cons of such an idea which, on the surface, seems so preposterous. On a deeper level, the idea is rather tragic. Finneman, we learn, is actually fearful of dying and of being alone. In a sense, having himself stuffed would be a way of cheating death, of somehow managing to live on. After a heartfelt and tearful talk with his wife, he finally realizes his request cannot be honored by anyone.

(NOTE: Harold Gould is extremely touching as Finneman, so desperately searching for a way to continue on after he has stopped breathing. The actor hits his usual high marks, and that is high praise indeed.)

Kelsey, Abby, Markowitz and Anthony Cavelli, toy company president, put their heads together to stop a hostile takeover of the man's business. A meeting with the aggressor, Gordon Stern, turns volatile. Stern actually shoves Cavelli, who suffers a mild heart attack as a result. Kelsey immediately jumps on this, declaring that charges of criminal assault and a civil suit will be filed against Stern by the end of business that day. They are successful in their efforts, scoring a major coup for the firm. McKenzie is so impressed over this and their past achievements, that he puts out an offer for Kelsey and Markowitz to become partners.

While working on his court case, Kuzak has discovered that Van Owen will be getting married in a few days. At the ceremony, Kuzak shows up in a gorilla suit and manages to tell Van Owen he loves her. She is so touched by this action that she leaves her fiance at the alter and everyone in attendance in shock.

Episode Six

"Slum Enchanted Evening"

Written by Marshall Goldberg

Directed by Gregory Hoblit

Guest Stars: Barbara Bosson (Stacey Gill), Karen Austin (Hillary Mishkin), Bernie Hern (Judge Schroeder), Dean Devlin (Christopher Sullivan), Richard Gates (Kevin Crenshaw), Bill Marcus (Glen Maroni), Maggie Han (Sandy), Shelly Gibson (Nancy), Roger Nolan (Lenny Krupp), Joanna Frank (Sheila Brackman), Cynthia Harris (Iris), Mario Van Peebles (Andrew Taylor), Diane Vincent (Kiosk Girl), Priscilla Pointer (Judge Pehlman), Phyllis Applegate (Ida), Michael Lear (Tim Noah), Lawrence Lowe (Driver #2), Julianna McCarthy (Frances Clifford), Andre Rosey Brown (Driver #1), Josh Clark (Ron Mitchell), Sandra Gary (Ann), Brian Scott (Jerry), Bill Kalmenson (Judge Salamunovich), Tom McGreevey (Mr. Albert), Grant Moran (Mr. Finney), Helen Siff (Mrs. Brantley), Palmella D'Pella (Mrs. Fields), Ernie Orsatti (Stunt), Beau Van Den Ecker (Stunt), Alan Oliney (Stunt), Carmen Argenziano (Neil Robertson), Bruce French (Brian Mellor)

Kuzak's client is broadcast journalist Stacey Gill, who was fired from her station because, according to her, she did a story on her breast surgery in which she bared a breast on the air. On the stand, she claims that her former employer, Barrett Broadcasting, actually *told* her to do the story, and responded by firing her. Their lawyer, Neil Robertson, counters this claim with the simple statement that her ratings were dropping. On television nothing is more important than the ratings; therefore they had no choice but to drop her.

The curiosity of Sifuentes is piqued when he notices a large number of people coming to visit the firm's new clerk, Jeffrey Sullivan. His curiosity turns to anger when Brackman confronts him about $300 worth of messenger bills, which he claims to know nothing about. Eventually he confronts Sullivan with his belief that he's dealing drugs. While Jeffrey admits to using the messenger service repeatedly without permission, he insists he is completely innocent of the drug charge. Victor ultimately is proven correct when Jeffrey attempts to sell drugs to an undercover narcotics officer and is busted. Iris wants to tell McKenzie "I told you so" regarding the young man, but he warns her not to.

Becker's problems begin at the staff meeting, where he announces that Hillary Mishkin will not be paying him any money from her divorce settlement, but rather from the profits of her film. Brackman is more vocally opposed to this method of payment than anyone. While Hillary and Becker embrace whenever they can, they try to lay out the film's promotional campaign.

Ann Kelsey and Stuart Markowitz are asked to become partners, but each of them have to come up with $87,000. For Stuart this is no problem, but Ann simply cannot afford it. Stuart offers to loan her the money, pointing out that he can easily afford to do so, and her love for him grows even more.

Former McKenzie-Brackman associate Andrew Taylor shows up at the firm, representing the people living in an apartment building owned by Douglas Brackman. To put it mildly, this building is a slum within a slum, equipped with peeling paint, heat that doesn't work, rusty pipes and rats of various sizes. Brackman, as is his wont, could care less, refusing to part with the money needed to improve the building, despite the fact that a judge has ordered Brackman to pay damages of $25,000 to each family within 10 days. Andrew counters with a lower settlement that the tenants would accept but Brackman again refuses, emphasizing that he'll let the system work for him and keep the issue tied up in the courts for years to come.

That night Brackman is grabbed by two men and forcibly taken to the rat-infested building, where he sees first hand the horrors that tenants have to live with daily. Taylor is there and Brackman says he'll take care of the damages, never having imagined things could be so terrible.

(NOTE: Up until this point, Alan Rachins has portrayed a very ruthless Douglas Brackman. All the man cares about is the bottom line and the expenditure of money, for whatever reason, is something he doesn't feel comfortable with. Thanks to Andrew Taylor, though, this hard exterior melts away when he is taken out of the comfort of his plush office and thrust into the horrible environment of the tenants.)

Episode Seven

"Raiders of the Lost Bark"

Written by David E. Kelley

Directed by Jan Eliasberg

Guest Stars: Barbara Bosson (Stacey Gill), Carmen Argenziano (Neil Robertson), Priscilla Pointer (Judge Pehlman), Bruce French (Brian Mellor), Grant Moran (Albert Finney), Joe Dehman (Sam Wiener), Karen Austin (Hillary Mishkin), Harry Caesar (Dwight), Mario Van Peebles (Andrew Taylor), Patricia Huston (Hilda), Cathy Paine (Wendy Bryant), Kevin A. Diffis (Clerk), Niles Brewster (Upton Weeks), Michael Fairman (Judge Doug McGrath), Starr Gilliard (Reporter #1), Kevin Roberts (Reporter #5), Cam Clarke (Reporter #4), Janet MacLachlan (Erica Tuckman), Edward Earl Rue (John Washington), Kim Murdock (Reporter #2), Alec Murdock (Reporter #3), Tara Zucker (Cindy Helms), Vince Irizarry (Peter Brosens)

On the office front, Markowitz gives Kelsey a check for $87,000 to buy her way into the firm. Meanwhile, Hillary Mishkin is thrilled by the reviews that

Striking out on her own, lawyer Abby Perkins, portrayed by Michele Greene, confers with a tough customer.

Benny Stulwicz, portrayed by Larry Drake,
is the beloved, hard-working,
developmentally-disabled mail room clerk.

her motion picture, *Rosebush,* is getting, while Becker is hurt when she announces she's involved with another man. Arnie goes through some serious self-pity.

Sifuentes gets suckered into taking one of Kuzak's no-win cases (dog bites man), and turns it into a victory. This allows him to take Kuzak's leather chair as the result of a wager they made at the outset.

Brackman, who is dissuaded from quitting the firm because of lack of respect from the partners ("You have to earn respect, Douglas," says McKenzie, "not command it."), meets with Andrew Taylor to arrange the sale of his apartment building.

Michael Kuzak meets with Cindy Helms, friend of Stacey Gill and secretary at Barrett Broadcasting. She has an important piece of evidence which will help in Gill's case against the station. Later, during trial, Barrett Broadcasting president Brian Mellor testifies that Gill was fired because the ratings for her newscast dropped significantly following her treatment for breast cancer. Although Kuzak is able to turn a research analyst's testimony in a way that favors Gill, it doesn't look all that promising for a verdict to go their way. The station makes a settlement offer but Gill holds out. She claims she wants the case to be decided by a jury, so that the station will never be able to do to anyone else what they did to her.

Surprisingly the jury decides in favor of Gill and awards her $1.3 million. During questions from the press following the verdict, Kuzak learns that Gill signed a book contract predicated on a jury decision, which is why she refused to accept the settlement offer. Kuzak feels completely used, and tells Grace Van Owen so when the two of them are alone in his apartment. She finds it difficult to feel sorry for him, knowing that he undoubtedly would

take the case again if he had the opportunity. She asked if he was any more used than Sifuentes was when Michael tricked him into taking the dog-bites-man case?

(NOTE: Barbara Bosson, who portrayed television journalist Stacey Gill, is the wife of series creator Steven Bochco. She appeared on such other Bochco productions as Hill Street Blues, Doogie Howser M.D., Hooperman *and* Cop Rock, *serving as a series regular on the latter two.)*

Episode Eight

"Gibbon Take"

Written by John Schulian

Directed by Sharron Miller

Guest Stars: Mimi Kuzyk (A.D.A. Marilyn Feldman), John Hancock (Judge Armand), Dean Devlin (Jeffrey Sullivan), Josh Clark (Ron Mitchell), Erica Yohn (Crazy Katy Flaherty), David Sage (Judge Hofheinz), John D. Lewis (Waiter), Anne Haney (Judge Travelini), Denise Crosby (Joan Turtletaub), Harry Caesar (Dwight), Denise Latella (Cop #2), Tom Hodges (Not Kuzak), Bibi Besch (Corrinne Dupree), Eddie Zammit (Garth Turtletaub), Ben Cooper (J. Howard Tucker), Liam Sullivan (Trustee Jarrett), William Anderson (Lt. Aldrich), Kim Murdock (Reporter #2), Richard Gates (Kevin Crenshaw), Kyle Scott Jackson (Cop #3), Don Cheadle (Julian Tatoon), Don Diamond (Trustee Lloyd), Thomas Ryan (Sid Hershberg), Albert Ash (Waiter Steve), Terry D. Seago (Not a Cop), Tamra Naggar (Moderator), Charles Wedon (Cop #1)

Grace Van Owen watches in horror as her opposing counsel, Sid Hershberg, attacks his own client, Julian Tatton, while the man is on the witness stand. As a result, Hershberg is held in contempt.

E
P
I
S
O
D
E
S

Sifuentes has been assigned the case of former McKenzie-Brackman clerk Jeffrey Sullivan, arrested on drug charges. Sullivan, despite Victor's recommendations, refuses to plead guilty. His hopes are to be a lawyer some day, and such a conviction would effectively end that dream. Next Sifuentes turns to Assistant District Attorney Marilyn Feldman, asking that she reduce the charges against his client. She refuses, citing a prior case in she had come up against Sifuentes.

The case goes to trial and the arresting officer, Ron Mitchell, takes the stand. It quickly becomes apparent that the incriminating cocaine is missing. As there is no evidence, the charges against Sullivan are dropped. Feldman accuses Sifuentes of stealing the evidence to protect his client and he responds by announcing he's filing a slander suit. Later, it's discovered that a court clerk had taken the cocaine for himself, which results in Feldman having to apologize to Sifuentes and ask that he drop the slander suit.

He agrees to do so, provided she make a public apology and give him her grandmother's rocking chair, which sits in her office. *(Too bad they dropped this little character quirk of Sifuentes'. The idea of his bargaining for people's chairs is a wonderful one).* That night, Jeffrey Sullivan shows up at the firm to retrieve cocaine he left behind. Abby catches sight of him and calls the police. Just as they and Sifuentes arrive, Jeffrey throws the drugs under the janitor's floor cleaner, thus destroying it. Sifuentes' response is to throw Jeffrey out of the office before he does something they'll both regret.

Van Owen, in the running for a judgeship, withdraws from the race when her former fiance, Kevin Crenshaw, humiliates her in front of the press and her peers by making sure they know she is the woman who left him at the alter for a man dressed in a gorilla suit.

She tells Kuzak she needs some time alone, but this is short-lived as the two are consumed by their love for each other.

Abby handles a divorce case in which a child is being used as a bargaining chip. She lets both sides have it for taking a child and manipulating him in such a way. Still with no idea where her own son is, she can't believe they could be so cruel. This outburst ultimately works for her, causing the divorcing parents to end things more amicably.

(NOTE: Michelle Greene does a nice turn here as Abby. Thus far she's been a hard-working, shy character who is forced to take the rotten things that life has thrown her way. Here, though, we get to see her explode with all the pent-up frustration she's been feeling.)

Ann Kelsey meets with trustees of the Meriwell Trust. It seems the late Mrs. Meriwell wanted her estate to go the homeless of Beverly Hills. Trust lawyer J. Howard Tucker points out that there are no homeless in Beverly Hills; therefore they want to use the money in the trust to erect a park. Kelsey goes out of her way to prove that there are indeed homeless people in Beverly Hills and eventually finds Crazy Katy, a bag lady from that city. Kelsey points out to Tucker that there are many more like Katy who will be brought before the jury if the trust doesn't reconsider its intentions. The trust eventually sees Kelsey's viewpoint, and agree to set up a soup kitchen in Mrs. Meriwell's name.

Katy is furious, saying that this is no help to her. She doesn't want to live in a shelter. She needs money, nothing more. Kelsey, in her opinion, is a user, just like everyone else in society. Ann is devastated, but at least there is a silver lining on her particular dark cloud. So impressed was the firm with her handling of the case, that McKenzie returns her check for $87,000. They have waived her fee to become a partner. She and Markowitz go out for a romantic dinner.

(NOTE: The episode was written by John Schulian, former story editor of Wiseguy *and supervising producer of* Midnight Caller. Star Trek *fans should note the appearance of two familiar actresses. Bibi Besch (Corrinne DuPree) played Dr. Carol Marcus in the motion picture* Star Trek II: The Wrath of Khan, *while Denise Crosby would go on to portray Security Chief Tasha Yar in the syndicated television spinoff,* Star Trek: The Next Generation. *)*

Episode Nine

"The Venus Butterfly"

Directed by Donald Petrie

Guest Stars: Gloria Rossi (Mrs. C. Troutman), Linda Phillips (Mrs. D. Troutman), Martina Finch (Mrs. F. Troutman), Laurel Schaefer (Mrs. G. Troutman), Debbie Zipp (Mrs. E. Troutman), Bobbi Jo Latham (Mrs. J. Troutman), Peter Frechette (Christopher Appleton), Cec Verrell (Angela Sipriano), Ben Frank (Mr. Walters), Lew Palter (Judge Leon Ruben), Edith Fields (Mrs. Cramer), Joe Mays (Foster Troutman), Cary Pitts (Jury Foreman), Tina Chappel (Reporter #1), Tom Tully (Reporter #2), James Arone (Dr. Wakeland), Tracee Lyles (Rosemary Beachy), Keith MacKechnie (Morgue Attendant), Stanley Kamel (Mark Gilliam), Sela Ward (Lynette Pierce), Milt Oberman (Dr. Warren Hensel), Phyllis St. James (Reporter #3), Felton Perry (Lester Tuttle)

Stuart Markowitz is given the polygamy case of Foster Troutman, representing one of the man's 11 wives, Angela Sipriano. Arnie Becker suggests that all of the wives be brought in to solidify their case against Troutman. Shortly thereafter, eight Mrs. Trout-mans arrive at the firm, each amazed at the other's existence. The deceit being made perfectly clear, all are more than willing to help. Later, Troutman's lawyer asks Becker and Markowitz to go as easy as they can with her client. Becker agrees as he has developed a sexual interest in her.

In an effort to gain a fuller understanding of the man's situation, Markowitz goes to jail to meet with Foster and is surprised to find someone who is far from the most attractive of men. During their conversation, Troutman tells him that he's always loved women and they've always loved him, thanks to the ultimate sexual secret: the Venus Butterfly. Appreciating Markowitz taking the time to talk to him, Troutman tells him the secret of the Venus Butterfly by whispering it in his ear. We never see the case go beyond this point, but Markowitz demonstrates the Venus Butterfly to Kelsey, and she is pretty blown away by it, begging him to show it to her again.

Van Owen is involved in a case in which Christopher Appleton shot his homosexual lover because the man was dying of AIDS and he wanted to put him out of his misery. During a particularly heartfelt session on the stand, Appleton details exactly why he killed his lover and *everyone*, including Grace, has tears in their eyes. Despite this, her job is to prove he is guilty. She emphasizes that he purchased the shotgun used in the murder three weeks before the incident took place, proving that it was premeditated. The jury agrees, finding Gilliam guilty of murder in the first degree. This is not a victory that she is proud of.

(NOTE: This episode represents one of the first episodic shows to deal with AIDS in such a way. There are no slams against the homosexual lifestyle; just an honest look at the pain of someone dying.)

Abby is told that the body of a dead child matching Eric's description has been found in the morgue. She and Kelsey race down there, only to be told that the paper work has not been finalized and they will have to come back the next day. Both women are furious. They return and are horrified to learn that through a clerical error, the body of the child was mixed up with that of another and cremated. Abby breaks down in tears, wishing she knew one way or the other if Eric was dead.

Episode Ten

"Fry Me to the Moon"

Directed by Janet Greek

Guest Stars: Jeanne Cooper (Gladys Becker), Peter Frechette (Christopher Appleton), Stanley Kamel (Mark Gilliam), Lew Palter (Judge Leon Rubin), Michael Rougas (Maitre d'), Sela Ward (Lynette Pierce), Jerry Taft (Bartender), Duke Moosekian (Cop #1), Jay Arlen Jones (Cop #2), Benjamin Jurand (Prisoner), Mort Sertner (Judge #2), Kim Joseph (Judge #3)

Van Owen brings up the Chris Appleton case with the man's attorney, Mark Gilliam, and provides him with some written information on AIDS stress syndrome. Armed with this material, it's quite possible that Appleton can get a new trial. Unfortunately Judge Ruben does not see this way, and turns down the request. Seeing no alternative, Gilliam claims that he was incompetent in his representation of Appleton, which leaves Ruben to free Appleton on bail pending his final ruling regarding a new trial.

Becker is asked by his mother to represent her in a divorce from his father. At first he's shocked, but then finds himself torn down the middle. His father can't believe he'd choose his mother over him; she feels the same way about her soon-to-be ex-husband. Thanks to

Roxanne's help, Arnie finally decides he will not represent either of them. Let them settle their own differences! Rox is rewarded with a bouquet of flowers.

Kuzak attempts to get rapist and murderer Jimmy Petrovek freed from jail and excused from the death penalty because, despite the fact that he is indeed guilty of the rape and murder of a pregnant woman, the police department did not have probable cause to arrest him. The argument is a convincing one and six appellate judges agree to drop the charges for this reason.

Shortly thereafter, Kuzak is processing the paperwork, filled with reservation over what he's doing. Is he really just turning a killer loose on society again? That night, Van Owen informs him of her disappointment in the effort he made to get Petrovek back on the streets. There is no time to consider this as Kuzak learns from a phone call that Petrovek was killed while trying to rob a liquor store.

Episode Eleven

"El Sid"

Written by Jacob Epstein, Marshall Goldberg & David E. Kelley

Directed by Allan Arkush

Guest Stars: Kenneth Tigar (Clarence O'Malley), Ellen Blake (Herself), Curt Wilmot (Randy Heidegger), David Cloud (Guy), Arnold Turner (Murray), Ron Fassler (Another Red Player), Howard Goodwin (Robert Scanlon), Damita Jo Freeman (Nina Emmons), Mary Gregory (Judge Pendleton), Simone Lazer (Waitress), Thomas Ryan (Sid Hershberg), Gary C. Stevens (Cop), Richard Stanley (Dekay), Jamie Wagerman (Clerk), Bruce Kirby (D.A. Rogoff), CCH Pounder (Judge Roseann Robin), Paul Bartel (Judge Daytona), Barry O'Neill (Eric Perkins), William Hubbard Knight Robinson (Referee), Boyd Gaines (Jim Perkins), Jerry Har-

din (D.A. Malcolm Gold), Pete Ernaut (Mover), Wally Rose (Manager)

Sid Hershberg, last seen punching out his own client, comes to Michael Kuzak and asks him to take over some of his cases so that he can take time off to get his act together. Michael reluctantly agrees, sensing that Sid in clearly moving over the edge. The pressure of defending the low lifes of the world is finally getting to him.

The first case involves Nina Emmons, a woman accused of attempted murder. Kuzak learns that police broke into her apartment in pursuit of her ex-boyfriend and she used a firearm to protect her children. One of them, the youngest, was killed in the cross-fire, but the police actually pressed charges against her. Kuzak tries to get her out on bail, but the price is much too high for her to afford. Feeling that she is an unfortunate victim in this case, he lays out the money himself so she can spend Christmas with her children. This done, he goes to visit Sid, who has been placed in a psychiatric ward. Sid is delighted to hear what Kuzak did for Nina Emmons.

Van Owen is reprimanded by her superior, District Attorney Bruce Rogoff, for her "manipulation" of the Appleton case. In retribution, she is placed on night court duty for an indefinite period. This becomes truly horrible for her when she learns that Judge Daytona has no intention of closing shop early on Christmas Eve.

Attorney Clarence O'Malley comes to the firm to tell Abby that he knows where Jim and Eric are and that Jim is willing to return the child if all charges against him are dropped. Becker doesn't like this idea, but Abby, so desperate to be reunited with Eric, hastily agrees. This leads to a courtroom, where Judge Robin receives Becker's request that all charges be dropped against Jim Perkins.

Immediately afterward, in the court hallway, Abby sees Eric and puts out her hands to hug him. Eric hesitates a moment, slowly approaches and begins to pummel the stunned woman before running back to his father. Eric, we will eventually learn, was told that Abby didn't want him anymore and told Jim to take him away.

(NOTE: Great final moment, and your heart can't help but go out to Abby Perkins. After all this time of questioning whether her little boy is alive or dead, she learns the truth and is quite literally slapped in the face.)

Episode Twelve

"Sidney, the Dead-Nose Reindeer"

Written by William M. Finkelstein

Directed by Jonathan Sanger

Guest Stars: David Dunard (Sgt. Horace Flynt), Fred Morsell (DeAngelo), Howard Goodwin (Robert Scanlon), Campbell Scott (Officer Clayton), Cynthia Harris (Iris), Maria Melendez (Janette Brauer), Ian Abercrombie (Gunther Hall), Thomas Ryan (Sid Hershberg), Darrell Larson (Tim Stanton), Robert Costanzo (Vinnie La Rosa), Boyd Gaines (Jim Perkins), Damita Jo Freeman (Nina Emmons), Barry O'Neill (Eric Perkins), Ellen Blake (Elizabeth Brand), Yana Nirvana (Gisela Radford), Rebecca Forstadt (Waitress), Jerry Butler (Rabbi Breindel), Christine Healy (Maureen Stanton), Teddy Siddall (Lurline Connors), Richard McGonagle (Stunt Busboy #1), Jeff Cadiente (Stunt Customer #2), J.P. David (Stunt Busboy #2), Tom Rosales (Stunt Customer #1), Michael Holden (D.A. George Handleman), Mary Albee (Stunt), Ronan O'Casey (Gregory Northrup)

Ann Kelsey is given the case of Gunther Hall, who has filed suit against Atwood-Wade, claiming the corporation stole his highly original tea bag invention. Gunther believes this invention will represent his one moment in history, and he refuses to allow anyone to rob him of it. Kelsey puts private investigator Vinnie La Rosa on the case and he comes back with information that Atwood-Wade is throwing out files which may be pertinent to the case.

Bags of garbage are brought to Kelsey's office, and she and LaRosa go through each bag. They find enough material to prove that the company did, indeed, steal the invention from Gunther and Atwood-Wade has no choice but to settle.

Becker handles the divorce of Tim and Maureen Stanton. Arnie is attracted to Maureen—particularly after her husband has described her as such an incredible lover—but Tim is such a nice guy that he doesn't want to hurt him. It's only a short matter of time before the couple does end up in bed, only to have Tim walk in on them. Becker is consumed with guilt until Maureen tells him Tim set them up together. It's the kind of thing that turns him on.

Abby gets a Christmas present in the form of Jim Perkins dropping Eric off at the house so that mother and son can share Christmas together. This time, Eric is overjoyed to be united with Abby.

Kuzak continues to work on the Nina Emmons case, and begins by questioning Sergeant Flynt, who has absolutely no sorrow for the death of the woman's daughter, Sarah. Another officer, Clayton, admits to being extremely nervous and trigger-happy when he saw Nina's weapon. While this is going on, Kuzak decides to see how Sid, who has been released from the psychiatric ward, is handling his workload. Sid delivers a powerful closing argument for his client, and ends the session by taking a gun from his briefcase and blowing his own brains

out. Kuzak, as well as the rest of the courtroom, is stunned.

Shaken, Kuzak goes back to Nina Emmons and tells her the police department has agreed to drop charges against her if she will drop the wrongful death claim she's filed. In his opinion, she ought to fight them, but Nina would rather put it behind her and stay with her family. The barest possibility of a guilty verdict is too powerful for her, as she could not handle the thought of being away from her loved ones for a prolonged period of time. A settlement is reached and Kuzak goes to Sid's funeral. Sadly, only a few people show up to pay their respects. Alone with Van Owen that night, he breaks down, racked with tears because there wasn't a single person who had anything to say about Sid—not even himself.

(NOTE: In this closing scene, Harry Hamlin brings forth Michael Kuzak's pain in such a natural way that you can't help but feel for him. He is like a child being cradled in Van Owen's arms, and it's a touching moment. Highly unusual for a leading man to be seen as quite so vulnerable.)

Episode Thirteen

"Prince Kuzak in a Can"

Written by Jacob Epstein & David E. Kelley

Directed by Rick Wallace

Guest Stars: Milton Seltzer (Judge Hood), George Cromwell (Sandy McPeak), Christopher Darga (Detective Zacchino), Dan Lauria (Joseph Sears), Michael Holden (D.A. George Handleman), Myrna White (Mrs. Fields), Teddi Siddall (Lurline Connors), Robin Gammell (Judge Englander), Maxine Stuart (Ellen Perle), Evan McKenzie (Thomas Canfield), Christina Rich (Jessica), Ellen Blake (Elizabeth Brand), Larry Welch (Salesman),

Grant Heslov (Andrew Putnam), Richard Dunn (Not Sears), Karl Anthony Smith (Technician), Lew Saunders (Guard), Marilyn Faith Hickey (Not Sandy), Ben Kronen (Gene Kahan), Charles Davis (Gray Fox Merithew), Nancy Burnett (Judge Forstenzer), Jennifer Rhodes (D.D.A. Gylkowski), Murray Leaward ("Gray Fox" Fox)

Victor Sifuentes is representing Andrew Putnam, an 18-year-old who used his computer abilities to access telephone company records to save his friends some money. Judge Englander agrees to drop all but one of the charges against him. Ironically, the firm's new phone system continues to break down and it's Sifuentes' suggestion they allow Putnam to take a crack at it. He does so and everything is soon in fine working order. Putnam's luck seems to be getting better, in fact, when he and Roxanne hit it off and they eventually go out on a date. They end the evening by sleeping together, despite the age difference between them.

Kuzak, having a hard time shaking Sid Hershberg's suicide, decides to take the man's various cases and it becomes obvious to everyone but him that the pressure is getting to be too much.

The first action is a hit-and-run case involving one Joseph Sears, who suggests that his elderly aunt lie to create an alibi for him. As soon as the words are out of the elderly woman's mouth, Kuzak asks to be excused from the case, but Judge Hood refuses the request. Not accepting this ruling, Kuzak takes himself off it. He is held in contempt and placed under arrest for his troubles. Sifuentes offers to help him with the extended caseload he has taken on and Kuzak accepts. Van Owen visits Kuzak in jail and comes to realize just how much pressure he has been under. She is the force that provides the light at the end of the tunnel for him.

Ann Kelsey pursues Cromwell Aircraft as a client, meeting with company president George Cromwell several times, once over dinner. Cromwell is so impressed with her ideas that he decides to have McKenzie-Brackman handle his legal affairs, provided that Ann Kelsey is his personal lawyer. She is happy to accept. This settled, Cromwell tells her he's attracted to her. Kelsey makes it clear she is involved with someone else—although it's also pretty clear that she finds him attractive as well. Viewing all of this from the outside is Stuart Markowitz, who finds himself growing more jealous with each meeting Ann has with the man.

(NOTE: Dan Lauria (Joseph Sears) is perhaps best known as Jack Arnold on ABC's The Wonder Years.)

Episode Fourteen

"The Douglas Fur Ball"

Directed by Donald Petrie

Guest Stars: Milton Selzer (Judge Hood), Grant Heslov (Andrew Putnam), Robin Gammell (Judge Englander), Jeff Feringa (Clerk), Clayton Martinez (Young Lawyer), Peter Kevoian (D.A. Aoli), Patricia Huston (Hilda), Christopher Carroll (Maitre d'), Sarah Abrell (Lisa Weston), Sandy McPeak (George Cromwell), Fran Bennett (Judge Johnson), Maurice Marsac (Waiter #1), Gloria Dorson (Receptionist), Curt Wilmot (Randy Heidegger), Duane Whitaker (Process Server), Monty Bane (Randolph Simpson), Joanna Frank (Sheila Brackman), Daniel Ziskie (Michael MacLeish), Terrence Beasor (Desk Sergeant), Jack Jozefson (Arresting Detective), Robert Crow (Uniformed Cop)

As Sifuentes brings Jeffrey Putnam in for sentencing, he is surprised to find that the 18-year-old was exactly correct in his prediction of what that sentence would be: six months probation and 80 hours of community service. Later he handles a robbery case involving a Hispanic and accuses Judge Englander of being prejudiced against minorities. He demands a new trial. Englander takes Sifuentes into his chambers and declares he is one of the most liberal judges on the bench. However, he says, if there is even the barest possibility of prejudice, he will indeed remove himself from the proceedings. He does give Victor something to think about: the majority of his clients are Hispanic. What does that say regarding his own priorities?

Markowitz grows more intensely jealous of the Kelsey/Cromwell situation and he tries to undermine Ann's autonomy in the situation. He later apologizes. She accepts, but when she meets with Cromwell in her office, Stuart barges in, looking for a misplaced tax book. Later, she goes to trial for Cromwell, proves victorious and he takes her to dinner. The night is capped off with a kiss and we see Markowitz watching from his car. The next day he confronts her with what he saw and she is furious with him. Not only is he jealous, but his mind is manifesting all kinds of paranoid delusions.

In counselling, Douglas and Sheila Brackman, who have been having problems for quite some time, discover that both of them have been involved in numerous extra-marital affairs. This out in the open, they reconcile and decide to give their marriage another go.

McKenzie, armed with a writ from the Court of Appeals, shows up at the jail and has Michael Kuzak freed. Judge Hood lashes out verbally at McKenzie for manipulating the system, but later apologizes to the firm's senior partner during lunch. He announces that he wants to retire from the bench and offers himself as a partner to McKenzie-Brackman. All Leland can do is bring it to the partners for a vote.

Ultimately they vote in the negative, which infuriates Hood. Finally McKenzie tells him the truth: his general attitude is so negative there is no way he will be anything more than a hindrance to the firm's activities. At episode's end, McKenzie is called because Judge Hook has been arrested for bribery.

Episode Fifteen

"December Bribe"

Written by John Jay Osborn, Jr.

Directed by Janet Greek

Guest Stars: Milton Selzer (Judge Morris Hood), Elizabeth Norment (Estelle Friedland), Pamela Kosh (Delores Kirby), Michael Holden (D.A. George Handelman), Liz Torres (Judge Linda Ruiz-Quinones), Sandy McPeak (George Cromwell), Jeff Allin (Scott Gottlieb), Alec Murdock (Reporter #1), Kimberly Beck (Nancy Tritchler), Michael Fairman (Judge Douglas McGrath), Patricia Huston (Hilda), Chip Johnson (Gordon Alport), Richard LaFond (Waiter), Ellen Blake (Elizabeth Brand), Cynthia Harris (Iris), Susan Wheeler Duff (Monica Alport), Grant Forsberg (Bartender), John McCann (Raymond Lloyd), Rocco Dal Vera (Reporter #1), Guy Christopher (Paul Glansman), Kerry Stein (Attorney Smith), Robert Beuth (Attorney Jones), Nadine Berger (Anchorwoman), Dakin Matthews (Stanley Kunin)

McKenzie visits Judge Hood in jail, telling him the district attorney's office is willing to drop all charges if Hood resigns from the bench. Not liking the advice, the man decides to get another lawyer. Eventually Hood does resign, on the evening news, and McKenzie realizes that the man's pride could not allow him to step down simply because McKenzie had asked him to.

Also on the McKenzie front, he has been asked by Raymond Lloyd, a senior partner at Marshall Taft's New York law firm, to merge their two organizations. McKenzie rejects the idea, saying the partners would never go for it. He does casually mention it at a staff meeting and everyone takes him to task for not having given them the chance to vote for themselves. A vote does follow, the tally being 3-3. McKenzie votes yes to break the tie.

Two members of the New York firm show up to check out the McKenzie-Brackman offices, and their discussions are all devoted to creating efficiency, with no discussions of the people aspect of the business. Finally, the partners vote *not* to go forward with the merger.

In terms of the 3-3 vote, Markowitz confronts Kelsey on this, saying the only reason she voted for the merger was to put distance between them. Since they first got involved, he claims, she has been thinking of ways to keep them apart. Now he's going to make it easier on her, by severing the relationship. Recognizing the validity of his words, Kelsey dives straight into their relationship, asking if they can check into a hotel so Stuart can once again demonstrate the Venus Butterfly. He's delighted to oblige.

Abby handles her first court case, defending a woman named Delores Kirby, charged with constantly harassing her daughter-in-law. She initially tries to get the charges dismissed, but Judge Ruiz-Quinones refuses. The case goes to trial with Mrs. Kirby verbally attacking her daughter-in-law in front of the jury. Abby loses the case and is reprimanded for poor preparation. It is not the most auspicious of starts.

Episode Sixteen

"Beef Jerky"

Written by Jacob Epstein & David E. Kelley

Directed by Helaine Head

Guest Stars: Mark Withers (Dr. Glasband), Suzanne Collins (Mrs. Brophy), Sheryl Lee Ralph (Renee Quintana), Kim Myers (Patty Brophy), Michael Collins (Mr. Brophy), Bill Marcus (Glen Maroni), Hartley Silver (Professor L'Hommedieu), Eileen T'Kaye (Jury Foreperson), Bruce Kirby (D.A. Rogoff), James McDonnell (D.A. Berenbaum), Bernie Hern (Judge Schroeder), Patricia Wettig (Carolyn Glasband), Brian Byers (David Mullane), Annie Abbott (Judge Neiman), Peter Speach (Bailiff), Gary Armagnac (Harry Pass), Michael Mitz (Dr. Christie), Michael Holden (George Handleman), Barry O'Neill (Eric Perkins), Paul Tompkins (Floyd), John Pinero (Medic), Marabina Davila (Juanita), Lauren Woodland (Kelly Brophy), Tony Frank (Lavanchy), Milton Selzer (Judge Morris Hood), Robert Firth (Bartender), Ann Blessing (Reporter #1), Tom Ashworth (Reporter #2), Ernie Orsatti (Stunt), Michael Fairman (Judge Douglas McGrath), Stanley Kamel (Mark Gilliam), Lew Palter (Judge Leon Rubin), Peter Frechette (Christopher Appleton), Paul Bartel (Judge Daytona)

Van Owen's delight at returning to day court is tempered by her first case: the theft of bull semen. The trial begins with the testimony of Professor Philip L'Hommedieu, who describes the process of gathering bull semen. Judge Schroeder calls Grace and opposing counsel into his chambers, where all three of them burst out in laughter. This leads to a discussion of how the semen was stolen, and the witness, Eugene Lavanchy, accidentally knocks over the last remaining specimen of semen. It ends with the jury finding Leonard Bauer guilty of theft and the audience got to view an enjoyable, light story.

Becker resorts to the lowest tricks he can think of to prove that Dr. Glasband has been cheating on his wife, but when the wife. discovers that her husband's lover is her own sister, she freaks out, purchases a gun and tries to kill him. Arnold is racked by guilt, but everyone is sure he'll soon recover; he always does.

Sifuentes handles the case of a family who lost a son in an accident involving their car and a truck. The boy's sister, Patty, blames herself for his death, and is racked by guilt. The family settles out of court with the trucking company.

Episode Seventeen

"Becker on the Rox"

Written by William M. Finklestein

Directed by Mimi Leder

Guest Stars: Randy Brooks (Malcolm Taggert), Charles Quertermous (Juror #6), Myrl Svela (Juror #7), Annabella Price (Bridget Reynolds), Russ Marin (Dr. Schwartz), Christina Johns (Candy), Charles Summers (Judge Pope), Larry Drake (Benny Stulwicz), Lesley Woods (Mrs. Stulwicz), Ellen Blake (Elizabeth Brand), James McDonnell (D.A. Berenbaum), Nancy Burnett (Judge Geraldine Forstenzer), Diane Vincent (Juror), Basil Hoffman (Baldred Townsend), Walter Bobbie (Joel Zweibel), Michael Fairman (Judge Douglas McGrath), Grant Forsberg (Bartender), Patricia Wettig (Carolyn Glasband), Mark Withers (Dr. John Glasband), Brian Byers (David Mullane), Michael Holden (D.A. George Handleman)

When McKenzie-Brackman is given the account of Northland Pharmaceutical, Kuzak's first assignment is to handle an action taken by five people impaired while using several of the company's products. When he meets with their counsel, Kuzak must deal with a consulting firm completely wrapped up in making sure that he looks just right for the television cameras that will be in the courtroom. Michael is incredulous, believing Northland might be better off taking the time to focus on a settlement rather than on the trappings of the electronic age. After the trial has received some attention, and therefore free publicity for the company, Northland gives Kuzak permission to settle with the complainants.

Kelsey asks Markowitz to help with her taxes. She is so disorganized that Stuart can't believe it, and they end up in frequent fights. They eventually make up when Stuart asks her to sell her condo and move in with him. This, he says, is for tax purposes and because he loves her and wants to wake up next to her each morning. Ann considers this for a moment, and happily agrees.

Roxanne asks Arnie for a proper cost of living wage increase, but Becker refuses, saying the firm won't allow it and that he can't afford to take it out of his pocket. Rox continues to bring the subject up and, getting no satisfaction, threatens to quit.

Abby handles the case of the retarded Benny Stulwicz, who was tricked by a supposed friend into stealing things. Judge Forstenzer, after watching Benny on the witness stand, decides that he honestly did not know he was stealing, and dismisses all charges. A victory for Abby!

(NOTE: This episode introduces Larry Drake as Benny Stulwicz, a retarded man who eventually becomes a series regular. So good a job does Drake do as Benny, that much of the television audience spent a great deal of time believing he really was retarded. Looking for change of pace roles as of late, Drake starred as a demented Santa Claus in an episode of HBO's Tales From the Crypt *and as the villain in* Darkman.*)*

Episode Eighteen

"Fifty Ways to Floss Your Lover"

Written by Jacob Epstein & David E. Kelley

Story by Steven Bochco & Terry Louise Fisher

Directed by Mimi Leder

Guest Stars: Jane Windsor (Meredith), Gail Ruscetta (Sam), Jack Stehlin (Court Clerk), Philip Reeves (Dr. Bassett), Ebbe Roe Smith (Daniel Bridges), Julie Ow (Dental Assistant), Frederick Coffin (Bill Novicky), Richard Galli (Foreman), Felton Perry (Lester Tuttle), Annie Abbott (Judge Neiman), Gregory Wagrowski (Elber), Dorothy Sinclair (Mrs. Lundstrum), Dore Keller (Harkavy), John Hancock (Judge Armand), Bruce Kirby (D.A. Rogoff), Laura Esterman (Gloria Rheinhold), Martin Azarow (Robert Sylvia), Jennifer Holmes (Jocelyn Pennebaker), Pat DiStefano (Emergency Room Doctor), Ivy Broya White (Mrs. Cramer), Jeffrey Alan Chandler (Gun Clerk), Burton Collins (Judge Hurwitz), Damon Hines (Punk), Jason Ross (Anthony Mosha), Matt Butler (Marshall #1), Dana DiCiano (D.A. Eve Fleinganhamer), Robert Picardo (Joe Dumphy), J.W. Smith (Walt Buckner), Ann Blessing (Reporter #2), Rocco Dal Vera (Reporter #3), Kim Murdock (Reporter #4), Wren Brown (Marshall #2), Cal Gibson (Reporter #1), Michael Holden (D.A. George Handleman), Richard LaFond (Waiter), Barry O'Neill (Eric Perkins)

While on jury duty, Roxanne continues to try to get a raise out of Arnie, who is totally unresponsive. Her resolve is somewhat shaken when he brings in a beautiful temp, but ultimately she refuses to back down and Becker agrees to pay her out of his own pocket. To add insult to injury, as far as he's concerned, he can't get to first base with his temp, and understands the reason when the woman's lesbian girlfriend shows up.

Racked with pain from a terrible toothache, Sifuentes goes to see the incredibly beautiful dentist, Dr. Jocelyn Pennebaker. After taking care of his pain, she wonders if Sifuentes would be willing to take on a malpractice suit that's been filed against her. He agrees, and soon learns that the former patient claims that Jocelyn planted a radio receiver in her mouth—the reason she constantly is picking up radio waves. They go before Judge Nieman, who quickly realizes that Jocelyn did not plant a radio receiver, but rather that the woman is crazy. The case is thrown out of court. Appreciating all he's done for her, Jocelyn invites Victor back to her apartment and the two start to make passionate love. Jocelyn, in the midst of passion, pulls out some tooth floss and starts cleaning his teeth. Sifuentes makes a quick departure, much to the woman's anger.

Grace Van Owen is questioning people regarding gang leader Walt Buckner. Her first witness is Anthony Mosha, who witnessed Buckner killing a police guard. The second, Daniel Bridges, saw Buckner rape and stab a young man in prison. The defense tries to tie Buckner's criminal activities to a troubled childhood, but nobody buys it. Buckner is given the death penalty and as he's hauled out of the courtroom, he threatens Van Owen's life. District Attorney Bruce Rogoff recommends that she buy a gun for protection, but she refuses to slip down to that level.

Later, while Grace is walking through the courthouse, a young boy pulls a gun and shoots her, the bullet winding up in her shoulder. She slumps to the floor, more shocked than anything else. She asks for and receives a gun permit and goes to a shop to purchase a weapon. Holding the pistol, Van Owen recognizes the horrible power in her hand and decides *not* to buy it.

(NOTE: This story perfectly portrays the character of Grace Van Owen, a

true believer in working within the system but tempted to go beyond it. Ultimately though, upon studying the ramifications of such an action, she decides she can't go through with it.)

Episode Nineteen

"The Grace of Wrath"

Written by William M. Finklestein

Story by Steven Bochco & Terry Louise Fisher

Guest Stars: Adam Arkin (Robert Kendall), Bruce Kirby (D.A. Rogoff), Keith Mills (Judge Stone), Patricia Huston (Hilda), Haunani Minn (Judge Sheps), Calre Wren (Shannon), Amy Van Nostrang (Nancy Schacter), Scotch Byerley (Foreman), Gary Blumsack (Stuart Zaplin), Terrence McNally (Dr. Paul Wooden), Henry G. Sanders (Judge Lowry), Tim Perot (Axel), Damon Hines (Kevin Rollins, Lizzie Maxwell (Jury Foreperson), Stephen Godwin (Leon Schachter), Jennifer Basey (Rita Steinhauser), Alfred Dennis (Izzy Hersch), Marta DuBois (Gwen Fuller), Bob Ari (Mr. Athony), Lionel Smith (Steven Norman), Wendy Cutler (Kahn)

It's Bruce Rogoff's opinion that Grace Van Owen should take some time off, but she refuses, noting that she has to attend the hearing of the teenager who shot her, Kevin Rollins. The public defender requests that the charge be reduced because Van Owen wasn't seriously hurt, but the judge agrees with her attorney that it's lucky she's alive at all.

After this, Grace starts cutting unbelievably lenient deals with criminals, and is called on the carpet by Rogoff, who claims that fear, not rational judgement, is clouding her mind. She is assigned to desk work for an indefinite period. She turns to Kuzak for support, but he points out that Rogoff is only trying to help her. Van Owen tells him off, declares that she doesn't need any-

one's help and then bursts into tears.

Sifuentes defends Israel Hersch, accused of growing marijuana in his backyard. Although Victor loses this case, juror Gwen Fuller finds herself very attracted to him and asks him out to lunch. Later, while Sifuentes is in an empty courtroom, Gwen approaches and asks him to put her on the stand to be "cross-examined". He plays along with this until she starts ranting and raving about being a slut and having to be punished. Shaking his head, Victor leaves the courtroom. The man is definitely not on a lucky streak with the ladies.

Kelsey handles a malpractice suit involving a plastic surgeon. His patient, Rita Stenheiser, claims that following surgery, her face was in severe pain. Kelsey proves that her pain is more psychological than anything, as improving her looks did nothing to prevent the divorce from her husband, who married a much younger woman.

Episode Twenty

"Sparky Brackman R.I.P. ?-1987"

Directed by Paul Schneider

Guest Stars: Tess Harper (Patricia Pittman), Priscilla Pointer (Judge Pehlman), Nick Cassavettes (Richard Bertrand), Warren Kemmerling (John Anthony Keris), Robert Costanzo (Vinnie La Rosa), Enid Kent (Joan Cherundolo), Patricia Huston (Hilda), Dinah Lenney (Receptionist), Rod Britt (Jury Foreman), John McGhan (Court Clerk), Whitney Kershaw (Lori Abrams), Elena Stiteler (Fran Winston), Cheryl Checcetto (Marietta Havens), Joseph Oliveri (Draftsman), James Hornbeck (Harkness), Ellen Blake (Elizabeth), Michael Holden (George Handleman), Clyde Kusatsu (Judge Masouka), Kevin Roberts (Reporter #1), Kim Murdock (Reporter #2), Frederick Ponzlov (Window Washer

*Blair Underwood portrays
agressive lawyer Jonathan Rollins.*

Jimmy Smits portrays Victor Sifuentes, a street-smart lawyer with top-notch skills and a deep commitment to justice.

#1), RCB (Window Washer #2)

Brackman's neighbor, Keris, files a lawsuit against him, claiming that his dog, Sparky, is a public nuisance. Abby takes the case and is very noticeably coached by Brackman in the court room. So much, in fact, that Judge Masouka orders him to quiet down. While the judge thinks Brackman should try to keep Sparky's noise level down, he does not consider the dog to be a public nuisance and throws the case out of court. Keris, it would seem, will not accept this so easily. First, Brackman's car tires are slashed. Then Sheila calls him at the office to tell him Sparky is dead. In response, Brackman goes to Keris' office and punches him out. He's arrested for this and has to be bailed out by Kuzak.

Kelsey and Markowitz go at it again, because she keeps rejecting offers for her condo. Stuart sees this as nothing more than her desperate attempt not to be completely committed to him. She sees that this is true, and finally does sell the condo.

Kuzak is handling the date rape of Lori Abrams, who claims that basketball star Richard Bertrand was the perpetrator. A settlement is offered, but she refuses to accept it. Bertrand's attorney, Patricia Pittman, puts Lori on the stand and introduces an old boyfriend who claims that Lori at first said no to the idea of sex, and then agreed to it. This, Pittman argues, is Abrams' pattern, so the charge of date rape is not a valid one. Next, Kuzak cross-examines Bertrand and reveals photographs of Lori's bruised thighs, indicating that she had been handled much more forcefully than passion would dictate. The jury finds in favor of Abrams, but only awards her one dollar. Kuzak, who wasn't entirely convinced himself of her innocence, suggests she accept this, but Lori is determined to find a lawyer who will more strongly support her needs. He is filled with guilt when a woman named Fran Winston steps forward and states that she, too, was raped by Bertrand.

Episode Twenty-One
"Oy Vey, Wilderness"
Directed by Mimi Leder

Guest Stars: Daniel Davis (Ron Messer), Cynthia Harris (Iris Hubbard), Melissa Weber (Clerk), Steven Williams (Detective Sgt. Phipps), David Wiley (Judge Peck), Kevin Bash (S.M.P.D. #2), Mimi Kuzyk (Marilyn Feldman), Joey Gian (Aaron Fein), Warren Kemmerling (John Anthony Keris), Lise Cutter (Lucinda Bonner), Michael Tulin (Marvin Hessen), George Skaff (Ramon Trilfa), Judy Jean Berns (Virginia Zeppoli), Michael Simms (Franco), David P. Lewis (S.M.P.D. #1), Lizzie Maxwell (Bailiff), Luke Askew (Ron Messer), Bill Cakmis (Abbot)

Kuzak and Markowitz tackle the case of Ron Messer, whose boat—and therefore his source of living—is mistakenly confiscated by the IRS. Agent Marvin Hessen matter of factly declares that Messer is a major drug dealer, and that the tax he owes is based on illegal activities he was involved in. Kuzak argues that there is no proof, but Hessen won't listen to anything he has to say. Kuzak, with IRS counsel Virginia Zeppoli, eventually goes before Judge Paul Peck, who expresses regret about the circumstances but says he has no choice but to side with the IRS.

Sifuentes attempts to get the assault charges against Brackman dropped, and this is agreeable provided the two parties meet and try to work out their differences. To this end, Brackman arranges a luncheon at the office. During the meal, Keris starts to choke on some food. At first, Brackman does nothing, gloating over the man's near demise and comparing it to Sparky's death, but he performs the Heimlich maneuver to dislodge the jammed food. As soon as Keris starts breathing again, he claims to have a broken rib and threatens to sue Brackman over it. Even the man's lawyer won't proceed, believing that Brackman and Keris are punishment enough for each other.

On the personal front, Stuart Markowitz and Ann Kelsey set out on a camping trip that turns out to be nothing less than a disaster. Summing up the entire experience is the moment when Kelsey uses leaves to wipe herself and happens to catch poison ivy.

More seriously, Grace's depression over getting shot becomes more intense and she turns to alcohol and tranquilizers as an escape. Kuzak tries to help her, but she is totally unwilling to let him do so. It comes down to his threat to leave her if she doesn't seek some help. At episode's end, she leaves the apartment, hoping Michael will be there for her when she gets back. For the moment, she has to find herself again.

Episode Twenty-Two

"Pigmalion"

Directed by Shelly Levinson

Guest Stars: Millicent Martin (Arlene Sabrett), Felton Perry (Lester Tuttle), Cynthia Harris (Iris Hubbard), Michael Tulin (Marvin Hesen), Melissa Tufeld (Nurse), Ellen Blake (Elizabeth Brand), Robert Del Sesto (Bailiff), Cherry Davis (Tonya), Luke Askew (Ron Messer), Pat Corley (Uncle Willard), Lee Garlington (Regina Furnald), Greg Mullavey (Gil Furnald), Charles Levin (D.A. Robert Caporale), Marc Tubert (Dr. David Koenig), Paul Bovino (Court Clerk), Richard Fancy (Norman Klein), T.J. Worzalla (Child), Lisa Kahofer (Kimberly Best), David J. Partington (Marshall Schulian), Mary Gregory (Judge Pendleton), Frank An-

nese (Bart Breinan), Stefanie Mason (Elizabeth Furnald), Sukey Smith (Waitress), Peter Willcox (Reverend Sivle)

The IRS finally admits to having messed up in the Ron Messer case and tells him he can have his boat back. Unfortunately, however, the bank insists on a payment from him before it's released. This is impossible for Ron as he has not been employed since the government took the boat. His response is to punch out a bank employee and Kuzak rushes to the jail to bail him out.

Van Owen works out her problems, recognizing the fact that she can't run away from the realities of life, and returns to Kuzak.

Arlene Sabrett meets with Becker, claiming that her husband, the host of the children's show *Uncle Willard's Animal Farm,* has been sleeping with one of the show's prize pigs. This whole situation would be laughable, if not for the fact that Arlene continues to interrupt Becker during considerably more serious divorce cases. It culminates when she drops off the pig in question so she can get her hair done. When this causes him to lose an important client, Arnie flips out, places the pig in Willard's hands and is promptly fired by Arlene. He couldn't be happier.

Sifuentes, assisted by Abby Perkins, takes on the case of Regina Furnald, who claims to have suffocated her young child with a pillow because she thought both she and the baby were on fire, and that placing the pillow on his face would stop the fire. Dr. David Koenig suggests that Regina might have been suffering from postpartum psychosis. District Attorney Caporale doesn't buy this at all, claiming that any such postpartum disease does not excuse the fact that she murdered an innocent baby. The woman's husband,

Gil, is called to the stand and he testifies that she had wanted to see a psychiatrist prior to the child's death, but they simply couldn't afford it.

Closing arguments are given and as Sifuentes and Abby wait for a verdict, they watch Regina get angry at her daughter, Elizabeth, and slap her across the face. The verdict is not guilty, although the judge orders Regina to undergo psychiatric evaluation. Abby attempts to persuade Victor that the outburst of anger they had seen is normal for any parent-child relationship, but he isn't convinced. Did they just get a murderer off the hook?

(NOTE: This storyline represents one of the first times the series would conclude with an ambiguous ending: was the client guilty or not? In this case, is there a chance that Regina will injure her daughter? A great moment that Victor Sifuentes instantly picks up.)

Her "skin condition" cleared up, Kelsey goes out for a romantic dinner with Markowitz, who proposes to her. When she says yes, he declares he wants to do it right away. They drive to Las Vegas for a quickie wedding. When the minister turns out to be an Elvis impersonator, they break up laughing and decide to leave and get married the proper way.

SEASON TWO

PRODUCTION CREDITS

Executive Producer: Steven Bochco
Co-Executive Producer: Gregory Hoblit
Co-Executive Producer: Rick Wallace
Producer: Scott Goldstein
Co-Producer: David E. Kelley
Supervising Producer: Terry Louise Fisher
Coordinating Producer: Phillip Goldfarb
Associate Producer: Bob Breech
Executive Story Editors: Jacob Epstein
Executive Story Consultant: William M. Finkelstein

REGULAR CAST

Harry Hamlin: Michael Kuzak
Susan Dey: Grace Van Owen
Corbin Bernsen: Arnold Becker
Jill Eikenberry: Ann Kelsey
Alan Rachins: Douglas Brackman, Jr.
Michele Greene: Abby Perkins
Jimmy Smits: Victor Sifuentes
Michael Tucker: Stuart Markowitz
Susan Ruttan: Roxanne Melman
Richard Dysart: Leland McKenzie
Blair Underwood: Jonathan Rollins
Larry Drake: Benny Stulwicz

Episode Twenty-Three

"The Wizard of Odds"

Written by David E. Kelley

Directed by Gregory Hoblit

Guest Stars: David Rappaport, George Coe, Laura Johnson, Kim Delaney, Ray Abruzzo, Arthur Taxier, Wanda DeJesus, Diane Delano, Lew Palter, Ralph Seymour, Jordan Charney

To aid charity, Becker allows himself to partake in an auction where men are the items up for bid. At first resistant to the idea, he eventually has a good time and is surprised—as well as flattered—when a beautiful woman named Nina Hollender wins him for $5,000. The two have a romantic dinner, and the evening ends with them in bed. Nina handcuffs Arnie to the bedpost so she can get her full $5,000 worth.

Ann Kelsey represents Dr. Peter Warren, a psychiatrist who did not report to the police that one of his patients, Elliot Robb, claimed he was going to kill Allison Tommey. Now, the victim's parents are filing a civil suit against him. Kelsey's argument is that he could not tell the police because it would betray doctor-patient privilege. Opposing counsel, Inez Santiago, puts Warren on the stand and tries to get him to admit that he's at fault, but the doctor refuses. Through further investigation, Kelsey is able to prove that Elliot Robb, in fact, did not kill Allison, and the charges are dropped.

In a private moment, Dr. Warren admits to her that he is the one who committed the murder. He emphasizes that Kelsey can't say anything, because it would violate attorney-client privilege. During dinner with Markowitz she says she can't get Warren out of her head and wants to do something about it. He reminds her there's nothing she can do.

Brackman gets the opportunity to be a temporary Small Claims Court judge and like everything else involving Douglas, he gets into the role a bit too much. His first case involves a foul-mouthed parrot.

The firm hires Jonathan Rollins as an associate, guaranteeing him a yearly salary of $72,500. McKenzie has faith that this young man will be worth the money, while Brackman thinks that such a salary will create resentment from the other associates. Then, counters McKenzie, they'll have to keep the issue quiet.

Victor Sifuentes represents James Peletier, the maker of pajamas which caught fire and permanently disfigured a 10-year-old boy named Kevin Talbot. While both Sifuentes and his client feel badly for Kevin, they don't feel responsible for what happened. Peletier makes what would seem a reasonable settlement offer, but Talbot's lawyer rejects it as being too low. It's at that moment that Sifuentes realizes he has come up against the legendary lawyer Mighty Mouse—Hamilton Schuyler, a dwarf who manages to manipulate juries for both himself and his clients.

The case goes to trial, and during Sifuentes' examination of a woman named Geraldine Walworth, Schuyler sets a pair of displayed pajamas on fire. Sifuentes immediately demands a mistrial. Judge Vance refuses, but gives Schuyler a stern warning on appropriate behavior. Putting young Kevin on the stand, Schuyler is told that the other children treat him like a leper. Sifuentes cross-examines and establishes that Kevin had spilled lighter fluid on his sleeve and then lit a cigarette. This is what caused the pajamas to burst into flames.

In a private moment with Judge Vance, Sifuentes argues that there is no evidence of a design defect in the clothing. Schuyler doesn't agree and argues the point until Vance says the trial will continue. Later, Sifuentes looks to make another settlement offer, but he finds his opponent hanging on a coat hook, being taunted by two men. Sifuentes scares them off and helps Schuyler down. They go back into court with Schuyler using his bruised and battered appearance as proof of how the freaks of society are treated. Judge Vance calls a recess.

(NOTE: A pleasant thing about this whole case is the relationship between Sifuentes and Schuyler. These two men, after different goals, have a true respect for each other. Jimmy Smits and David Rappaport play off each other wonderfully.)

Episode Twenty-Four

"Cannon of Ethics"

Written by Jacob Epstein

Directed by John Patterson

Guest Stars: David Rappaport (Hamilton Schulyer), Ray Abruzzo (Anthony Gianelli), Arthur Taxier (Dr. Peter Warren), Lesley Woods (Mrs. Stulwicz), Madlyn Rhue (Judge Wyatt), George Coe (Judge Vance), Caroline Williams (Mrs. Talbot), Robert Benedetti (James Peletier), Christie Houser (Woman Juror), Kim Delaney (Leslie Kleinberg), Laura Johnson (Nina Hollender), Jonathan Brandis (Kevin Talbot), David Milch (James Beaumont)

Victor Sifuentes puts Mrs. Talbot on the stand. The jury learns she left her apartment for 10 minutes and when she came back, her son, Kevin, was engulfed in flames. More questioning brings out the truth that she was gone considerably longer than 10 minutes and, that if she had been there, the tragedy might not have occurred. A juror screams out in defense of Mrs. Talbot and Sifuentes uses the moment to request a mistrial. Judge Vance has the juror removed, but will not declare a mistrial. James Peletier, manufacturer of the pajamas in question, agrees to pay the settlement that Schuyler originally asked, but now the attorney wants even more, which infuriates Sifuentes.

The jury eventually comes back with a $4.5 million verdict in favor of Kevin Talbot. In Vance's chambers, Sifuentes expresses his anger and Vance agrees, feeling there was no evidence to support the jury's decision. They were operating on pity, nothing more. He overturns the decision. Shortly thereafter, Schuyler asks Sifuentes if the original settlement offer is still possible. They agree to disuss the matter over dinner. During that meal, Schuyler admits that the idea of winning became overwhelming and that he did indeed lose track of his client's needs. Sifuentes nonetheless refers to him as a brilliant lawyer.

Becker has been missing for two days. By the time he returns to the office, without having called at all during the past 48 hours, Roxanne is a nervous wreck. Her apprehension turns to anger when told he spent two days with Nina, who he now feels deeply in love with. His joy starts to fade as soon as Nina says something about marriage. Suddenly the idea of commitment frightens him and he becomes cold to her until she breaks up, chastising him for not being man enough to have a mature relationship.

Abby meets with the mother of Benny Stulwicz. The woman is dying and remains concerned about what will happen to Benny once she's no longer around to protect him. Abby says she'll try to get him a job at the firm as a messenger. She brings it up to the partners and everyone seems to agree with the idea, although Brackman has certain reservations. These are put to rest when it's pointed out he will save a considerable amount of money on messenger expenses if they have someone in house to handle the responsibility. It's all the convincing he needs. Benny is hired.

Kelsey, still upset about Dr. Warren's confession of murder, goes to meet with elderly attorney Wendel Gleason. Gleason feels the best way to expose Warren is for him to violate attorney/client privilege with Kelsey. She adamantly refuses to allows him to put himself on the line in that way. The next day, Kelsey reads Gleason's announcement in the press and is angry. She goes to meet with him and is told that after having heart surgery twice, he feels the end justifies the means. Warren shows up at Kelsey's office, threatening to file a lawsuit against her. She strikes back verbally and effectively shuts him up, although there is a not so subtle threat in his words.

Episode Twenty-Five

"Brackman Vasektimized"

Written by Robert Cochran

Directed by Anson Williams

Guest Stars: Tovah Feldshuh (Lynn Palmer), Kim Delaney (Leslie Kleinberg), Diane Delano (Rhonda Vasek), Joanna Frank (Sheila Brackman), Ellen Blake (Elizabeth Brand), Reuven Bar Yotam (Joseph Ludlum), Kellie Overbey (Tammy Schiff), David Wakefield (Bill Tobias), Connie Needham (Denise Franklin), Robert Kim (Judge Ronald Kim Park), Joan Webb (Judge Helena Thompson), James Sutorious (Lyman Hatcher), Nicolas Coster (Brian P. Young), Bo Zenga (George Chernov), Frank Ashmore (Bruce Wellman)

While serving as a judge in Small Claims Court, Brackman becomes sexually involved with his bailiff, Rhonda Vasek. Meanwhile, Abby Perkins finds out Jonathan Rollins' salary and is furious. She goes to Sifuentes and tells him, suggesting they confront McKenzie together. Victor tells her, as politely as possible, he would rather fight his own battle. Hurt, Abby leaves his office. Later, Sifuentes meets with McKenzie and expresses his dissatisfaction. Either he gets a raise, or he quits. How much will it take to keep him? Since Rollins is getting $72,500, Victor wants $72,600. Smiling, McKenzie agrees. Shortly thereafter, Abby finds out about the situation and tells Kelsey she's going to make the same demand and threaten to quit. It's Kelsey's opinion she should not make the threat unless she's willing to follow it through. If Abby delivers an ultimatum, the odds are strong that they will let her go, Kelsey tells her.

Arnie Becker finds himself attracted to a new associate (what else is new?) named Leslie Kleinberg. Fearing she would be fired, she avoids any kind of relationship with him. Kleinberg is given the case of a man who saved the life of another man, but the latter's car plummeted over a cliff in the process. Now the savee is out to sue the saver. Through every bit of manipulation she can manage—including flirting with jurors—Kleinberg wins her case. The victory is bitter, though, and she decides to leave the firm. Arnie learns she is writing a novel about a law firm, and it clearly matches the people of McKenzie-Brackman. Becker reads it and wants to represent it for a percentage, which she agrees to.

Kuzak meets up with his ex-wife, Lynn Palmer, who he deserted years earlier. Seeing her again awakens some old feelings he tries desperately to deal with. At the same time, Grace Van Owen is furious that he never told her he had been married. She also is threatened by the potential renewed relationship that might develop between Michael and Lynn.

Kelsey represents Washington Pure Water Co. against Denise Franklin, who claims her son was born deaf and blind due to the fact that she drank from a well located next door to the company. Franklin's attorney, Lyman Hatcher, stops by Kelsey's office with a document that pretty much proves that the contamination could have occurred. In response, Kelsey goes to company CEO Brian Young and tells him about this. His reply is to settle for $3 million, because it would cost much more than that for them to clean up their dump site. Kelsey is sick over the entire situation.

In an act of desperation (albeit honestly felt), Kelsey brings Young the settlement papers, which have been amended to say he will clean up the dump site. If not, Kelsey says, she will go to the press with her findings. Young threatens to sue McKenzie-Brackman, but she announces she's quitting the firm, so he can't hold them liable. Not knowing if she's bluffing, he signs the paper. Kelsey hands her resignation in, but McKenzie, although not approving of her methods, rips it up.

Episode Twenty-Six

"The Brothers Grim"

Written by William M. Finkelstein

Directed by Michael Zinberg

Guest Stars: Jeff Silverman, Tovah Feldshuh, Sheila Larken, Maria O'Brien, Matt Landers, Marco Rodriguez, Bette Ford, Diane Delano, Ellen Blake

Benny Stulwicz's mother dies and the entire firm rallies around him in support, providing their love and friendship as a guide to the future.

Van Owen meets with Kuzak's ex-wife, Lynn Palmer, and discovers the woman still is interested in him. The lunch meeting ends with Van Owen feeling more threatened than ever, and she decides to move out of the apartment to get a break from Kuzak.

While making wedding preparations, Markowitz asks Kelsey to sign a pre-nuptial agreement, saying it's a requirement of his family's estate. She happily does so and he, in turn, rips it up. Seems he was testing her love and she passed with flying colors. Unfortunately for him, Kelsey doesn't like the idea of her love being questioned and she has him write up a new prenuptial agreement. She's going to sign it and he's going to have to live with the fact that he made her do it. Markowitz is a neurotic mess as a result.

When Brackman takes over a case his father had been involved in years earlier, he makes some surprising discoveries. They include the fact that the man had a mistress named Rusty Farrell and he has a half-brother named Erroll Farrell. McKenzie knew about this but was sworn to secrecy by Douglas Brackman, Sr. Brackman meets with Rusty and learns about his father's past. Then he meets with Erroll, who, it turns out, also is a lawyer. Excited, Brackman goes to see his office, and is disheartened to find it to be a seedy little place and his brother is even seedier. At first, Erroll is thrilled to have a big brother and it seems like the two of them are really going to hit it off, but it's only a short matter of time before Erroll tries to involve Brackman and his firm in a business scam.

Sifuentes represents Carmen Carillo, who had been raped at knifepoint in a bar while, unbeknown to her until later, police officer Carl Sackett sat in his seat and did nothing. Sackett's argument is that he had had several drinks and was afraid that he would accidentally shoot an innocent bystander. Sifuentes' cross-examination causes Sackett to go on and on about the dangerous situations police officers find themselves in every day. Later, we learn through the man's captain, Lee Reynoso, that there had been an incident where Sackett's partner was in trouble and he didn't return fire on a suspect. After closing arguments, the jury takes a recess. Sackett approaches Carmen and apologizes profusely to her, begging for her forgiveness. Carmen says she has no forgiveness for him. Shaking his head sadly, Sackett walks out of the courtroom. Moments later, he blows his brains out while in the men's room. A hell of an ending for one hell of a case.

Episode Twenty-Seven

"The Lung Goodbye"

Ever since the issue of the pre-nuptial agreement, Kelsey has been cold to Markowitz no matter what he tries to do to make amends. Finally he suggests that they see a therapist to work out their communication problems. They end up in the office of a married team of therapists, but while in the waiting room they hear the two screaming at each other in fury. Markowitz and Kelsey mutually agree to work out their own problems, and head off to a hotel to begin "sessions."

Kuzak represents Patrick O'Brien, a cigarette smoker suffering from emphysema, who has filed suit against Leheigh Tobacco. One of the people that Kuzak questions is Leheigh CEO Bradford Fredericks, a man in his late 60s, who smokes regularly. During the trial, Dr. Arthur Saxon testifies on behalf of Leheigh Tobacco, attempting to diminish the long-term effect of cigarette smoke. Kuzak makes it known to the jury that Saxon's research is funded by various tobacco companies, therefore he cannot be unbiased. When the verdict comes in, the decision is in O'Brien's favor, but he is awarded only $1,000. Kuzak suggests they appeal the decision, but Patrick would rather drop the issue and spend what's left of his life with his family.

Episode Twenty-Eight

"Auld L'Anxiety"

Written by Jacob Epstein, David E. Kelley and William M. Finkelstein

Story by Steven Bochco and Terry Louise Fisher

Directed by Nell Cox

Guest Stars: Jeff Silverman, Jesse D. Goins, Rosalind Cash, John Furey, Diane Delano, Zero Hubbard, Terrence McNally, Don Starr

The hypocrisy that can sometimes be "Judge" Douglas Brackman becomes apparent when he lectures a couple on the sanctity of marriage and a short time later continues his extra-marital affair with his bailiff. Erroll Farrell catches them in the act and the price of his silence is a bit of temporary working space at McKenzie-Brackman, so that he can cover up the seediness of his business.

In a rare move, McKenzie takes on a case dealing with age discrimination. Needless to say, he handles himself wonderfully and there's no doubt that his client, William Claflin, is in good hands. Claflin's boss, Dean Ackerson, is put on the stand, where he explains that Williams' performance had been slacking off, which is why he was fired. *Not,* he emphasizes, because of the man's age. McKenzie reads off Claflin's accomplishments over the past several years and effectively wins his case without a hitch.

Van Owen meets with Nonnie Sweet, a woman who no longer wants to testify to witnessing the murder of Tanya Drummonds at the hands of gang member Maurice Crimmins. Grace can relate to the fear that both she and her son Julius are experiencing, but she promises them police protection. Things don't go as planned, however, when Officer Milton Labine tells Van Owen that the Sweets can't be relocated. He promises to keep an eye on them during the trial. At that time, Van Owen questions Nonnie.

Afterward, the woman and Officer Labine walk down a courthouse corridor lined with gang members making nonverbal threats. That night, Van Owen is having drinks with Kuzak, when a television newscast announces that Nonnie has been killed. She rushes to the woman's home and faces the hatred of Julius. To make matters worse, the case will have to be dismissed because of Nonnie's death.

(NOTE: Once again we're given a perfect example of how working within the system doesn't always pay off. The character of Grace Van Owen is the perfect tool to demonstrate this as she is a member of the District Attorney's office.)

Episode Twenty-Nine

"Rohner vs. Gradinger"

Written by Jacob Epstein, David E. Kelley and William M. Finkelstein

Story by Steven Bochco and Terry Louise Fisher

Directed by Sharron Miller

Guest Stars: Clayton Rohner, Finola Hughes, Constance Towers, Joe Marinelli, Karmin Murcelo, Diane Delano, Joel Colodner, Jay Gerber, Joan Pringle, Jacqueline Scott

Having carefully considered his relationship with Rhonda, Brackman decides to break it off. She seems to accept this. Later, during a partners' meeting at McKenzie-Brackman, Rhonda suddenly bursts in and lashes out at him for having her transferred to another location, simply because he could not handle their relationship. "The things I let you do to me," she screams, mortifying Brackman in front of the others. In response, Brackman offers to resign, but McKenzie talks him out of it. Perhaps, though, it would be a good idea for Brackman to seek a marriage counsellor. As if things weren't bad enough, when Brackman goes to the men's room, Arnie Becker gives him a speech about AIDS, which makes him completely paranoid.

Kelsey's mother comes to town to meet Stuart for the first time and the woman deliver a constant barrage of anti-semitic remarks. He takes great offense to them, although at first he tries to ignore them. The woman apparently doesn't mean harm; the problem is her way of thinking. Things reach a breaking point during a party, when Stuart has had enough and retaliates by turning over a cabinet filled with expensive china. At episode's end, Kelsey states categorically that if it's a choice between him and her mother, her mother will lose.

Abby in involved in a case between two men, Rohner and Gradinger, who are battling over the rights to a muffin recipe. Meanwhile, Markowitz is fired by film producer Gordon Bass but, despite McKenzie's warnings not to, Rollins not only delivers the man's files to him, but puts on a cocky one-man-show that wins Bass back over to McKenzie-Brackman, provided that Rollins will represent him. Instead of appreciation, McKenzie voices his anger. If Jonathan should ever disregard his instructions again, he will be terminated. Also happening concurrently is Kuzak asking Van Owen to move back in with him.

Sifuentes gets trapped in an elevator with Lauren Sevilla, whose marriage is very seriously on the rocks. The two of them flirt with each other and she ultimately agrees to have dinner with him, despite fear of her husband, Armand. Sifuentes says the man won't harm her while he's around.

Kuzak represents spoiled actor Patrick Boyd, who punched a man named Ronnie Cevenko outside a restaurant. Police arrived moments later, found a vial of cocaine on Patrick and arrested him.

Kuzak is able to work out a deal where the charges against Patrick will be put aside if he enters a drug rehabilitation program. Unfortunately, Patrick won't admit that he has a drug dependency problem. He wants Kuzak to continue with the trial, during which he claims the cocaine was not his and that he does not take drugs of any kind. Patrick is found not guilty, but Kuzak feels no reason to celebrate. Later, he gets a phone call from Patrick, who has just been in a car accident, where cocaine was found on his person. Kuzak refuses to take the case.

Episode Thirty

"Goldilocks and the Three Barristers"

Written by David E. Kelley and William M. Finkelstein

Story by Steven Bochco and Terry Louise Fisher

Directed by Rick Wallace

Guest Stars: Caitlin O'Heaney, Finola Hughes, Diane Delano, Hildy Brooks, Tony Carreiro, Brett Porter, Bruce Kirby, Irene Ferris, Joel Colodner, Jay Gerber

Since Benny is feeling depressed, Becker decides to cheer him up by taking him on a Melrose Avenue shopping spree. By the time they're down, Benny is dressed like a fashionable man, but he doesn't feel comfortable in the clothing. Eventually Roxanne points out that he has to behave in a way that makes him happy, not Arnie. Soon he's back in his old clothes. Becker is disappointed but understands.

Brackman has convinced himself he has contracted AIDS and has a blood test. Two excruciating days later, he finds out the test came back negative. Trying to be a nice guy in a way that only he can do so, Brackman goes to see Rhonda, tells her of his joy of not having AIDS and suggests she not be so promiscuous in the future for fear of the disease herself. She punches him out.

Abby handles her case between Manny Rohner and Marty Gradinger so well the two have decided they will become partners again and they want her to be their in-house counsel. McKenzie is pleased, asking her to stay on at the same salary as Jonathan Rollins—$72,500. Abby says she has to think about it, but both of them know very well that she's going to stay on board.

Van Owen is handling the case of Jeanie Morris, who was sexually accosted by a trio of lawyers while delivering an erotic dance-o-gram. District Attorney Bruce Rogoff wants Grace to take things easy and work out a settlement so the careers of the three lawyers aren't ruined. That's an idea she can't live with and she leaves his office furious. During the trial, Grace examines Jeanie and opposing counsel shows the jury the outfit Jeanie wore during the dance. Despite the fact the defendants' lawyers are trying to put Jeanie on trial, she refuses to back down and change her charge against them.

When she returns to her office, the other workers in the D.A.'s office hire a stripper as a joke. Van Owen does not see the humor. Back in court, one of the lawyers, Delinsky, admits that they did touch Jeanie, but that was it. Van Owen pounces on this and destroys the man's credibility. A guilty verdict is delivered against all three lawyers, much to Van Owen and Jeanie's joy. Heading home that night, Van Owen sees Kuzak and tells him that they don't laugh enough in their lives. She brings a helium balloon into the apartment, the two of them take a "hit" and declare their love in distorted voices.

Episode Thirty-One

"Divorce With Extreme Prejudice"

Written by Joe Cacaci

Directed by Sam Weisman

Guest Stars: Finola Hughes, Jeff Silverman, Bernie White, Silvano Gallardo, Richard Coca, Douglas Dirkson, Gregory Itzin, Ray Girardin, Anne Haney, Bernie Hern, Joanna Frank, Patricia Huston, Ellen Blake

Brackman tells his step-brother Erroll that the man's days as blackmailer are over; he has told Sheila about his affair with Rhonda. Smugly he heads off to work. At the end of the day, Brackman comes home to find Erroll in bed with Sheila.

Sifuentes' romance with Lauren is going well, but as is often the case with the man's relationships, things go terribly wrong. He goes to her home for dinner and finds a group of police cars there. Heading inside, he's told that Lauren shot her husband to death when he threatened to kill her. The police believe it was murder, not self defense, and it's something that Sifuentes is giving serious consideration to as well. While the jury finds her innocent, he's not convinced and this effectively ends their relationship.

Van Owen is prosecuting Reuben Mercato, accused of murdering his father, Jose. He claims self defense and evidence of the scene does establish that there were bruises on his body. Reuben's mother, Vera, claims to having heard Jose threaten the life of their son. Why, Van Owen wonders, didn't she ever report this to the police? The jury doesn't believe the testimony, finding the man guilty of murder in the second degree. In a private moment with Kuzak, Grace admits she's going to try and get the sentence reduced.

Episode Thirty-Two

"Full Marital Jacket"

Written by Terry Louise Fisher and

David E. Kelley

Story by Steven Bochco and Terry Louise Fisher

Directed by Win Phelps

Guest Stars: Ray Abruzzo, Constance Towers, Tony Perez, Charles Frank, Penny Santon, Laurie Souza, Bill Wiley, Joanna Frank

Ann Kelsey and Stuart Markowitz finally tie the knot and getting there is an absolute comedy of errors. First off, they are fighting constantly, with Ann getting nastier and nastier as they get closer to the actual ceremony. During the ceremony itself, Sheila Brackman loudly announces that she wants a divorce from Douglas and walks out of the church. The clergyman performing the wedding is rather surprised to see that Kelsey and Markowitz are barely talking to each other, but he smiles broadly as their anger melts away to be replaced by the depth of their true feelings.

Benny is arrested for rape. Through tear-filled eyes, Benny pleads with the police to contact Arnie Becker, which they do. When Becker arrives, he's told that a rape victim identified Benny's photo. To make the case even stronger, Benny confessed. McKenzie tells Becker that they'll bail Benny out of jail, but he cannot work at the firm until he's cleared of all charges. In further discussions, Becker learns that Benny had been to a peep show, had seen a naked woman and touched his own penis when she instructed him to. He *did not* rape anyone, and thought he was in trouble for going to the peep show and touching himself.

Helping out, Kuzak goes to meet with the woman Benny had seen, and she corroborates the story. She'll help, but only if Kuzak can be sure she won't get in trouble herself. Panicking, though, the woman leaves the city. Judge Mason puts the victim, Jody Flood, on the stand and after listening to Benny's

Susan Dey portrays Deputy District Attorney Grace Van Owen.

Dave Meyer, portrayed by Dann Florek (left) consults with
divorce lawyer Arnie Becker, portrayed by Corbin Bernsen.

voice, she realizes he isn't the rapist. The only reason she said he was was because the police convinced her of the fact. The charges against Benny are dropped.

(NOTE: This represents one of the best Benny stories ever done on the series. Larry Drake does an incredible job and the plot seems to be an indictment of the way that youth—remember, Benny has the mental capacities of someone much younger—of today are "protected" from sex. More open discussions might prevent many of the unfortunate things that happen.)

Episode Thirty-Three

"Gorilla My Dreams"

Written by Jacob Epstein and William M. Finkelstein

Directed by Gabrielle Beaumont

Guest Stars: Charles Frank (Jimmy Markham), Penny Fuller (Cynthia Levine), Kate Zentall (Rita Seaver), Ellen Blake (Elizabeth Brand), Jessie Scott (Fox), Larry Cedar (Wilentz), Richard Jamison (Andy Globas), Vinny Argiro (Malvasi), Jandi Swanson (Katie Seaver), Steve Vinovich (Ken Seaver), Patti Johns (Lois Manfredi), John Lawrence (Reuben), Daniel Benzali (Judge Phillips)

Considering Benny's confusion over sex, as evidenced by his confession to a rape he didn't commit, McKenzie believes that someone should take him in hand and explain the facts of life. Sifuentes volunteers for the job when Becker hems and haws. They head for the zoo and start to discuss the birds and the bees when the janitor mentions that the male gorilla is going to be punished severely for injuring one of the female gorillas. Naturally, Benny gets all flustered, thinking that this is the kind of lesson he's going to get taught if he should ever hurt a woman.

Victor tries to calm him down and gets an idea. He asks McKenzie to use whatever connections he has to get the two gorillas reunited. According to Sifuentes, Benny is seeing himself through the gorillas' eyes and has to be shown that things can be all right. This is done and it seems to have the desired effect on Benny, who becomes convinced that even a retarded man can have a social life. Sifuentes suggests a social club for the retarded, which Benny says he will check out.

Roxanne is dating Jimmy Markham, an investment broker, who's been giving her various stock tips. In turn, she has been giving Ann Kelsey some advice and everyone is making some money out of the deal. Later, Markham is arrested right in front of Rox by members of the LAPD and FBI for securities fraud. Kelsey feels sick when Markowitz mentions that anyone who made money from Markham's information could be found liable.

Becker represents Ken Seaver, whose wife filed charges against him for sexually molesting their daughter, although the man denies this while on the witness stand. Seven-year-old Katie Seaver is led to Judge Phillips by her temporary guardian, Manfredi. The youngster is too frightened to give the judge anything useful. Considering the charges, he allows Katie to go home with Mrs. Seaver and will only allow scheduled supervised visits by Mr. Seaver. The next day, Mrs. Seaver runs to Becker's office and claims that Ken has kidnapped their daughter, adding in her hysteria that she made up the molestation story. Becker finds Ken and convinces him that returning the child would be the right thing to do. Judge Phillips considers the idea of placing Katie in a foster home, because both of her parents seem too unstable to be trusted.

Episode Thirty-Four

"Hard Roll Express"

Written by William Stadiem

Directed by Kim Friedman

Guest Stars: Rosalind Ingledew (Sandra Davis), Hildy Brooks (Sarah Kerwin), Mark Schneider (Eli Goldman), Bruce Kirby (D.A. Rogoff), Jerry Ayres (Stanley Niles), Fran Bennett (Judge Hilary Johnson), Sam Behrens (Charles Craft), Conchata Farrell (Lorna Landsberg), Craig Richard Nelson (Donald Kelly), Todd Jeffries (City Attorney Martin), Christine Rose (Gay Holloran), Jim Jansen (Geoffrey Bowers), Charles Frank (Jimmy Markham), Andrew Schneider (Alexander Emmanuel), Peter Kevoian (D.A. Aoli)

While Brackman engages in what seems to be harmless flirting with a woman named Sandra in a Japanese restaurant, he's suddenly arrested for solicitation. McKenzie comes to help, emphasizing that Brackman was reading selections—albeit suggestively—from the menu with Sandra. Recognizing the lack of hard evidence, the police drop the charges and officer Sandra Davis offers her sincerest apologies to Brackman. He accepts the apology, then asks her out to lunch.

Sifuentes defends food critic Lorna Landsberg, who is accused of committing libel when reviewing Emile's restaurant. The plaintiff's attorney calls food critic Geoffrey Bowers, who feels that Lorna's criticisms were malicious and unprofessional. Sifuentes is nonetheless able to establish that she had a right to publish her opinions. When Emmanuel enters the courtroom, he and Lorna get into a screaming match in front of everyone. The judge calls for a recess and, in a private moment, Emmanuel declares his love for Lorna. At that moment, Sifuentes realizes the entire scenario is the result of Lorna having been jilted by the man. She drops all charges and leaves the courthouse with Emmanuel, Sifuentes not quite believing what just happened.

Jimmy Markham expresses his fears to Roxanne; saying he could get through this thing provided she doesn't testify. Believing that Jimmy loves her, Roxanne agrees and tells Becker and Kuzak so. They try to make her see the reality of the situation—that Jimmy is conning her—but she won't listen to what they have to say. In the federal courthouse, Roxanne is put on the stand but refuses to say anything about Markham. As a result, she is held in contempt and taken to jail. Surprisingly, Roxanne is visited by Jimmy's live-in girlfriend, Gay Halloran, who thinks that Markham should get what he deserves and wants Rox to testify. Realizing she's been betrayed, she agrees to do so.

Meanwhile, at a local restaurant, Kelsey tells Markowitz that the Rolex she bought him was paid for by money gotten through Jimmy's stock tips. Markowitz doesn't think he can enjoy it anymore, but really doesn't have to think much about it when the couple is robbed by a so-called "Yuppie Bandit" just outside the restaurant.

Charles Craft, an old law school friend, meets Grace for lunch and tells her that he just started his own firm and would love for her to be a partner. She tells him she'll think about it. Van Owen turns to Kuzak for advice, but he says he can't make the decision for her. Next she goes to D.A. Rogoff to hand in her resignation, and he gives the impression he just doesn't give a damn. At episode's end, Van Owen goes back to Rogoff and hands in her badge. A moment later, the entire staff burst into applause and gives her a going-away party.

Episode Thirty-Five

"Beauty and Obese"

Written by Terry Louise Fisher & David E. Kelley

Directed by Sam Weisman

Guest Stars: Susan Peretz (Lynn Stetler), Sam Behrens (Charles Craft), Bruce Ornstein (John Trischuta), Kevin Dunn (Barry Braunstein), Martin Azarow (Christopher Rauseo), Bever-Leigh Banfield (Gina Westland), Matt Roe (Peter Lundstrum), Shawn Hoskins (Rosalie Baskin), Joe Kane (Brad Sanford), Diane Brodie (Ghost Woman), Susan French (Edith Lundstrum), Will Gill, Jr. (Foreman), Ellen Blake (Elizabeth Brand), Joe George (Judge Hogan Mueller), James Handy (John Vincent), David Selburg (Tim Langella)

Markowitz meets with Peter and Gail Lundstrum, who are beside themselves because their mother, an old friend of Stuart's, is leaving her $30 million estate to television evangelist Billy Bob Thomas. Markowitz goes directly to the home of the woman, Edith, who admits she is leaving the money to the preacher as a form of punishment to her children, who are extremely self-centered. When Markowitz pushes the issue, Edith agrees to tear up the will and write a new one.

Days later, Edith's new attorney, Barry Braunstein, contacts Markowitz and tells him Edith has died and left him her entire estate to do with as he sees fit. His plans are to give all the money to the children, but Kelsey argues the point that they don't deserve it. Markowitz meets with the lawyers for the children as well as Billy Bob Thomas and announces—after much fighting among everyone—that the $30 million will be divided between the children and charity.

Kuzak represents lawyer Lynn Stetler, allegedly fired from her firm because of massive weight gain. During the trial, Lynn states the reason she was fired, while opposing counsel argues that the weight had affected her private life as well, which in turn affected her ability to function in her job properly. For closing arguments, Lynn says she wants to represent herself. Although Michael is nervous about the idea, he agrees. Lynn is dead-on perfect; her summation brilliant. The jury finds in her favor and, amazingly, applaud her when the verdict is read.

Van Owen is asked by Charles Craft to speak to organized crime figure John Vincent about his nephew's criminal matter. She is totally against the idea, but Charles presses until she agrees to meet with him. During their meeting, Vincent is convincing about his nephew's innocence, and Grace is willing to read over the case. After a time, though, she realizes that she simply cannot take this case. Charles is angry about her decision, but is unable to change her mind. During dinner at a restaurant, Van Owen tells Vincent she will not take the case. His pleasant manner suddenly turns threatening, informing Grace that she really doesn't have much of a choice. *will* clear his nephew! At that moment, a busboy approaches, takes out a gun and kills Vincent right in front of Van Owen.

(NOTE: As you can well imagine, Grace Van Owen, the other customers in the restaurant and the audience at home all sit there with mouths hung open in shock. Powerful ending.)

Episode Thirty-Six

"Pettycoat Injunction"

Written by Steven Bochco, David E. Kelly, Jacob Epstein and William M. Finkelstein

Directed by Alice West

Guest Stars: Kelbe Nugent (Jamie Needham), Kim Miyori (Carol Koyama), Sam Behrens (Charles Craft), Charley Lang (Robert Alden), Daniel Greene (Jack Seiling), Roderick Spencer (Jack Debente), David Nieman

(Wino), Tom Mustin (Juggler), David Michael Sterling (Security Guard), Elena Michaels (Cashier), Susan Tick (Jeane Kasabian), Michael Fairman (Judge Douglas McGrath), Kim Murdock (Reporter), John Hammil (Detective Miller), Alec Murdock (Reporter), Paul Regina (Felix Echeverria), Ellen Blake (Elizabeth Brand), Douglas Dirkson (Judge Lyne), Paul Motley (Attendant), Greg Norberg (Detective Hamel), Heidi Hennessey (Ivy)

Van Owen confronts Charles Craft with the fact that gangster John Vincent was a silent partner in their firm. The only thing we see of her through the rest of the episode is when she comes to Kuzak's office to tell him not to be late for the dinner she's cooking.

The Yuppie Bandit who robbed Kelsey and Markowitz is captured by police. On the stand, the robber's lawyer, Echeverria, manages to get Kelsey and Markowitz to give different testimony of what took place that evening. Alden, the robber, claims he bought the Rolex watch from Markowitz and was having it appraised when he was arrested. Judge Armand finds him guilty of receiving stolen goods, but there is no jail time. Afterwards, Alden comes up to Markowitz and offers to trade Kelsey's wedding ring he stole for the Rolex. Markowitz agrees for sentimental reasons and schedules a time for the exchange. They start the swap and Alden is arrested. He is charged with perjury at the last trial.

Benny goes out on a date and things apparently don't go too well as he won't even talk about it. When the woman, Ivy, shows up at the office to give him some cookies she baked, Benny is downright rude to her.

Becker is handling actor Jack Seiling, who is suing his television producers because they made him dress up in female clothes on the air. In a sense, Seil-

ing argues, they have destroyed his appeal as an actor. Producer Jamie Needham disagrees and things get pretty rough between her and Becker. Amazingly, that night the two meet in the garage and kiss. All is revealed later on, when Becker tells the partners that the entire court case is a publicity ploy designed to boost ratings for Seiling's television series.

Everyone is absolutely furious with him, and McKenzie goes so far as to rip up the check Arnie received in return for "representation." Kuzak points out that as important as money is, the firm doesn't want any that's dishonestly earned. To drive home this point, the partners set up a prank in which Arnie is almost arrested for misuse of the legal process. Their point strikes home and Arnie drops the case, much to Needham's anger.

Episode Thirty-Seven

"The Bald Ones"

Written by Steven Bochco, David E. Kelley, Jacob Epstein and William M. Finkelstein

Directed by Tom Moore

Guest Stars: Ralph Bellamy (August Redding), Patricia Huston (Hilda), Susan Ann Connor (Dr. Julia Robbins), Philip Tanzini (Thomas Mullaney), Mike Garibaldi (Middle Age Attorney), Jeffrey Tambor (Gordon Salt), Priscilla Pointer (Judge Pehlman), Nan Martin (Mrs. Brackman), Penelope Helenick (Jeanette Wheeler), Merrit Olsen (Minister), Ralph Myering, Jr. (Eli Aaronsen), Earl Boen (Judge Walter Swanson), Leonard Stone (Judge Paul Hansen), Don Sparks (Russell Spitzer), Ray Wise (D.A. Walter Platt), Jeff Silverman (Erroll Farrell), Joanna Frank (Sheila Brackman), M. Scott Wilkinson (Charles Mosha), James Sweeney (Bartender)

The court appoints Kuzak to defend

Andy Prescott, who is accused of murder. Ironically, Van Owen takes on the case of Prescott's partner, Thomas Mullaney, who drove the getaway car in the mutual robbery. She and Kuzak start to lay out a court plan, but end up in bed, saving conversation for the morning.

Rollins is told to assist Abby in a civil suit involving Maygen Manufacturing and an unhappy stockholder. Opposing counsel attempts to turn the issue into a class action suit, but Judge Hansen turns the motion down.

Brackman's mother dies, and he is devastated. Erroll shows up shortly thereafter, demanding a piece of Mrs. Brackman's estate. Of course this angers Douglas, but he's willing to give the twerp some money just to get him out of his life. At the woman's funeral, Douglas is joined in the pew by another bald man, Gordon Salt, who claims to be his step-brother (and after seeing how the baldness in the family ran between Douglas, Erroll and now Gordon, the joke has become hysterical). Gordon, a psychotherapist, is in town on business and heard about Mrs. Brackman's death. He came to pay his respects.

Later, at a bar, Gordon seems truly compassionate and Douglas feels as though a real connection has been made. As Brackman discusses his marriage, Gordon expresses his intent to help him and Sheila work things out. The three get together, and Sheila really seems fascinated by what he has to say. At the end of a session that seems to go remarkably well, the three of them embrace, with Gordon's hand squeezing Sheila's behind.

In what is perhaps one of Sifuentes' most moving cases, he represents Jeanette Wheeler, who received only a fraction of what she should have in a civil suit. This is alleged to be because renowned lawyer August Redding didn't

push hard enough—his mental facilities were slowly leaving him. McKenzie, an old friend, tries reasoning with Redding, but the latter believes Wheeler was greedy in what she wanted and there was no way she could have gotten it. He went for an amount he knew opposing counsel would agree to.

During courtroom examination, Sifuentes discusses Redding with Dr. Julia Robbins, and Redding shouts out that he objects to the other lawyer's line of questioning. Later on, Sifuentes puts witness Eli Aaronson on the stand and he expresses the opinion that Redding was grossly negligent in his handling of the Jeanette Wheeler situation. Opposing counsel brings out the point that Aaronson had once lost a case against Redding, which would be motivation enough for him to be here testifying against him. Sifuentes' argument is that Redding failed to carry out even the minimal amount of discovery that should have been required in the woman's case.

Then, in one of the most emotionally powerful courtroom scenes we've seen yet, he repeatedly asks Redding simple questions, such as Sifuentes' own name, and it quickly becomes apparent that the elderly man is suffering from short-term memory loss. He can remember events from decades ago, but what he had for lunch that afternoon escapes him. Redding's lawyer asks Sifuentes to step outside so they can work out a settlement. Victor, who took no pleasure in this particular trial, is happy to do so.

(NOTE: Legendary actor Ralph Bellamy does a tremendous job as August Redding, touching the hearts of the jury as well as the television audience. Thanks to such films as Eddie Murphy's Trading Places, *this veteran actor finds himself back in business again with the modern audience. Jeffrey Tambor (Gordon Salt) is a well-known character actor who has appeared in*

more sitcoms than anyone could ever count.)

Episode Thirty-Eight

"Fetus Completus"

Written by Steven Bochco, David E. Kelley, Jacob Epstein and William M. Finkelstein

Directed by Gregory Hoblit

Guest Stars: George Coe (Judge Vance), Ray Wise (D.A. Walter Platt), Philip Tanzini (Thomas Mullaney), Earl Boen (Judge Walter Swanson), Jeffrey Tambor (Gordon Salt), Bette Ford (Rusty Farrell), Alexandra Johnson (Tracy Arnett), David Ralphe (Kevin O'Keefe), Aixa Clemente (Sherril Saulter), Julian Gamble (Clinton Eustis), Cecelia Garcia (Clerk), Babbie Green (Jury Foreperson), Richard Roat (Dr. Woodwin), Christian Slater (Andy Prescott), Joanna Frank (Sheila Brackman), Kenneth Kimmins (Dr. Lawrence), Tony Goldwyn (Chris Arnett)

Van Owen is asked by Assistant District Attorney Walter Platt to cop a murder two plea for client Thomas Mullaney. He drove the getaway car for Kuzak's client, Andrew Prescott, who committed a robbery and killed a man. She refuses. Platt puts Sherril Saulter on the stand and she identifies Prescott by the jacket he was wearing when he came out of the store that night. Clinton Eustis is called next, and he identifies the duo as fleeing from the scene of the crime. Van Owen wants Mullaney to testify, though Kuzak thinks it's a big mistake. Kuzak, who must do what he can to protect Prescott, does his best to destroy Mullaney's credibility once Van Owen calls him.

During recess, Kuzak tries to plea bargain but opposing counsel won't budge. Prescot tells Michael that if he's put on the stand, he'll tell the truth

about what happened. Once there, Prescot claims that the man in the store was dead before he even got there. Van Owen is angry, not quite believing that Kuzak would allow someone to go on the stand and commit perjury. The two deliver their summations, resulting in Prescot being found guilty of murder and Mullaney declared not guilty. Over drinks, Kuzak and Van Owen make up and Grace says she's going to take her old job back at the district attorney's office.

No sooner has Brackman declared his renewed love for Sheila than he comes to her loft and finds her and Gordon naked behind a pottery wheel. A screaming match turns to a throwing one, with Sheila hurling the pots she has fired. Eventually Sheila, Gordon and Brackman's two sons show up at McKenzie-Brackman to work out a settlement agreement with Becker. Arnie's bombshell at the meeting is that Gordon served time in prison for bigamy and, no matter how convincing he sounds, he does *not* have a degree in psychology.

Sheila and Gordon profess their love for each other and leave. With nowhere else to go, Brackman shows up at Rusty's house and she provides comfort. In fact, she provides entertainment by showing him some porno films she starred in when she was younger. Their evening ends with a session of love-making.

Ann Kelsey finds herself in a difficult situation that puts her head to head with Abby Perkins. Kelsey is trying to get a court order to have a child prematurely delivered despite the mother's opposition, because the woman is dying of leukemia. The unborn child could die if not delivered early. She and a Dr. Laurence meet with the administrators of the hospital over this issue, but are told that for legal reasons, they cannot back up her request for a court order. In civil court, Chris Arnett, husband of the pregnant Tracy, questions Laurence about the idea of his wife delivering early. Judge Vance promises that his ruling will come quickly.

At the hospital, Kelsey goes to see Tracy at the woman's request. Tracy begs her not to interfere in the birth of her child, but Kelsey points out that she's trying to ensure that the baby will live. Soon thereafter, Vance makes his decision: the child will be delivered. Chris Arnett actually strikes Kelsey physically. At episode's end there is some consolation in the fact that although Tracy died, the baby did live. Chris Arnett apologizes to Kelsey for his earlier outburst; then breaks down and starts to cry.

(NOTE: Christian Slater (Andy Prescott) has often been deemed a young Jack Nicholson by the critics. Film audiences probably know him best for his roles in Heathers, Pump Up the Volume *and* Young Guns II. *The Kelsey story also is torn right out of the headlines, as there had been a very similar case in which right-to-lifers interfered with a man's decision to prematurely have doctors remove his child from his comatose wife as it might be just the thing to revive her. The child was indeed removed and the woman did recover. A lawsuit is now pending between him and the right-to-life organization that interfered.)*

Episode Thirty-Nine

"Belle of the Bald"

Written by Steven Bochco, David E. Kelley, Jacob Epstein and William M. Finkelstein

Directed by John Pasquin

Guest Stars: Dan Hedaya (Michael Roitman), James McDonnell (D.A. Berenbaum), Paul Willson (Marty Adelstein), Tomas Truhillo (Brother), Anne Haney (Judge Traveleini), Jeff Silver-

man (Erroll Farrell), Bette Ford (Rusty Farrell), Lance E. Nichols (Clerk), Bill Cobbs (Webb Johnson), Bruce Kirby (D.A. Rogoff), Helen Stenborg (Mrs. Lucille Graham), Gregory Itzin (D.A. Angeletti), Jill Vance (Secretary), Kevin Scannell (David Murray), Teri Sheridan (Jury Foreperson), Laurie O'Brien (Megan Penny), Shelby Leverington (Dr. Klepp), James Avery (Judge Conover), Renata Scott (Megan's Mother)

Brackman once again proves his ridiculousness in matters of the heart by admitting to McKenzie that he's in love with Rusty. This makes Leland extremely uncomfortable, as he is well aware of Douglas Brackman Sr.'s relationship with the woman. A day or so later, Brackman calls Rusty and asks her out on a date. They go to an old-fashioned dance hall, have a great time and end the night in bed together. It's at that time that Erroll Farrell walks in on them.

Grace Van Owen is welcomed back to the district attorney's office, and is given a case which doesn't seem very auspicious. Her task is to prosecute golf player David Murray, who murdered a swan when things weren't going well on the golf course. Club member Lucille Graham is called to the stand and she describes exactly what transpired in gruesome detail. While being questioned by his attorney, Michael Roitman, David Murray tries to convince everyone in the jury that the swan attacked him and that he had to kill it in self defense. Next, Van Owen calls club caddie Webb Johnson, who describes a day when Murray teed up a bullfrog that croaked while he was attempting a shot. Following closing arguments, the jury finds Murray guilty. He is sentenced to community service and a year without golf.

Kuzak wants his client Megan Penny to plead temporary insanity in the murder of Wilfred Arguello, who had raped her but was not charged due to diplomatic immunity. At trial, Dr. Irene Klepp is questioned by opposing counsel and she explains that in her opinion, Megan was not insane at the time of the murder. By the same token, Kuzak gets the woman to admit that Megan is not a threat to society. Kuzak has Megan describe the events surrounding the rape and then delivers his closing argument. The jury's verdict is that Megan is not guilty of murder due to temporary insanity. As she leaves the courtroom, Arguello's brother shoots her to death and declares diplomatic immunity.

(NOTE: James Avery (Judge Conover) portrayed Winslow in the fantasy romance series Beauty and the Beast, *and is a series regular on* The Fresh Prince of Bel Aire.)

Episode Forty

"Open Heart Perjury"

Written by David E. Kelley, Jacob Epstein and William M. Finkelstein

Directed by Tom Moore

Guest Stars: Jeff Silverman (Erroll Farrell), Raye Birk (Judge Steven Lang), Jeffrey Tambor (Gordon Salt), Bette Ford (Rusty Farrell), Joanna Frank (Sheila Brackman), Cynthia Sikes (Judge Anita Ryan), Laura Bassett (La Wanda Buttle), Richard Fancy (Norman Klein), Irene Tedrow (Mrs. Crutcher), Lora Staley (Lisa Maynard), Peter White (Stanley Silverman), Richard Masur (Robert Boland), Tom Everett (Patrick Phillips), Joshua Smith (Geoffrey Brackman), Coleby Lombardo (Alexander Brackman)

Having found his mother in bed with Brackman, Erroll Farrell is hurt, angry and wants revenge. When Brackman takes Rusty to the Bar Association cocktail party, Erroll, acting as Sheila's lawyer, hits him with a subpoena. Brackman responds by trying to choke the life out of Erroll. McKenzie stops

the fight and Brackman departs. He tries making up with Erroll, but life doesn't get any easier when Sheila, Gordon and the two kids show up at the office.

Arnie Becker and opposing counsel Patrick Phillips appear before Judge Monica Ryan regarding a divorce issue and she denies a motion both men are seeking. Later, Becker overhears her talking to an attorney named Norman Klein about her pending divorce. When they get back in court, Arnie uses this as ammunition, insisting that Ryan excuse herself because she cannot be impartial while in the midst of her own divorce. Angry at the idea that Becker should think she would be biased, she nonetheless removes herself from the case. Interestingly, she goes to Arnie later on and asks him to handle her divorce. Together they work out a great settlement and Ryan is free. Soon thereafter, she and Becker become involved with each other romantically.

Stuart Markowitz and Jonathan Rollins take on the case of 74-year-old Katherine Crutcher. She lost her life savings to business manager Robert Bolland, who allegedly invested it poorly. Bolland's attorney, Lisa Maynard, points out that her client had been given power of attorney by Mrs. Crutcher. While on the stand, Bolland apologizes with all his heart for what happened. He feels terrible about poor Mrs. Crutcher, but there's nothing he can do about it.

In private, however, Bolland is a cold fish, not giving a damn about Mrs. Crutcher or any of the other people he's ripped off over the years. The way he looks at it, he can appeal the case for years to come and by the time it's settled, Mrs. Crutcher, in all likelihood, will be dead from natural causes. Markowitz can't believe this is happening. He turns to Rollins and tells him to go to work on Bolland as only he can.

Rollins does so, keeping Bolland on the

stand for hours at a time, going over the man's personal finances in minute detail. After this has gone on for an incredibly long time, Bolland suddenly falls from his chair, victim of a heart attack. Jonathan immediately turns his attention to the judge, insisting that in case of death, the proceeds of Bolland's life insurance policy should be applied to the trial. At a later staff meeting, Kelsey and Abby give Rollins a hard time for being so insensitive. Markowitz, on the other hand, defends everything that Jonathan did and points out he's the kind of lawyer that makes money.

(NOTE: An interesting character point. Cynthia Sikes, who portrays Judge Monica Ryan, played Susan Johnson, girlfriend to Arthur Bach in the comedy Arthur 2: On the Rocks. *Of course Jill Eikenberry, who portrays Ann Kelsey on the series, was cast as Susan in the original* Arthur.*)*

Episode Forty-One

"Leapin Lizards"

Written by Steven Bochco, David E. Kelley, Jacob Epstein and William M. Finkelstein

Directed by Michel Zinberg

Guest Stars: Martin Ferrero (Julius Goldfarb), Mitchell Laurance (Richard Mathers), Bruce Fairbairn (Bernie Lustig), Marilyn Faith Hickey (Sandy), Cynthia Sikes (Judge Ryan), Robert Davi (Dominic Simonetti), Daniel Benzali (Judge Phillips), Tom Lacy (Gene Strouse), Dann Florek (David Meyer), Jenny Sullivan (Janet Pearce), Jeannetta Arnette (Vickie Simonetti), Rob Neukirch (Paul Varga)

Kelsey represents Julius Goldfarb, an actor forbidden to appear in public as a super hero named the Salamander, because the copyright holder of the character is planning on doing a motion picture version starring a younger man. Goldfarb had played the wall-crawling hero on television for a number of years. During trial, opposing counsel Richard Mathers puts film producer Edmund Bates on the stand and the man claims Julius has made the Salamander a joke. It is not the kind of image they want to perpetuate in the new motion picture.

When Kelsey puts Julius on the stand, it's obvious he feels emotionally connected to the character he portrays and the significance he holds for his fans. When Mathers cross-examines him, he really lays in to Julius to the point where Julius stands up, strips off his outer clothing and stands before everyone dressed as the Salamander. He even tries scaling the walls via suction cups, but falls to the hard ground below. Mathers rests his case. Julius is taken to a cell at the state hospital, and Kelsey pleads with him to give up being the Salamander. If he doesn't, she emphasizes, he will be committed to a sanitarium by the court.

Markowitz informs Roxanne she is in serious financial difficulty, and probably will have to declare personal bankruptcy. The bank will not give her much of a loan and she asks Arnie to co-sign, but he turns her down because it will only put her in a deeper hole. That night Roxanne goes out with the wealthy and boring David Meyer, a direct mail salesman, and listens impatiently as he drones on about his business and how successful he is. Finally, she burst into tears and runs out of the restaurant, leaving a bewildered Meyer behind.

Becker goes to view Judge Ryan's court just so that he can be a bit closer to her. The case involves police officer Dominic Simonetti and his wife, Vicki, who is seeking a divorce. More and more comes out about their private life and her unhappiness, and we can see Dominic getting angrier. He pulls a shotgun out of hiding and orders the courtroom doors sealed. Dominic threatens to kill his wife or to kill Ryan, although the latter argues the point that by doing this he will be denying his children their father. Vicki is the one who is able to convince him to give up the weapon and let everyone go. After being so afraid of losing her, Becker tells Ryan that he's been frightened of commitments in the past, but he would like to give it a shot with her. Ryan is delighted.

(NOTE: Robert Davi (Dominic Simonetti) in recent years has starred in such films as the James Bond thriller Licence to Kill, Action Jackson, Die Hard *and* Maniac Cop 2. *He also appeared as mafia kingpin Albert Cirecco in four episodes of the cult TV series,* Wiseguy.*)*

Episode Forty-Two

"Chariots of Meyer"

Written by David E. Kelly, Jacob Epstein and William M. Finklestein

Directed by Win Phelps

Guest Stars: James Earl Jones (Lee Atkins), Dann Florek (David Meyer), Dian Gallup (Twins), Denise Gallup (Twins), Jill Vance (Judy), Ray Glanzmann (Young Man), Scott Lawrence (James Ray Edwards), Michael Fairman (Judge McGrath), Carmen Argenziano (Neil Robertson), James Tartan (Jury Foreman), Philip Sterling (Judge Cramer), Ellen Blake (Elizabeth), Lenka Peterson (Julia Clarent), Dan O'Herlihy (Vernon Kepler), Peter Hobbs (Steven Henderson), Nick Angotti (Walter Briles), Dana Sparks (Jennifer Kepler)

Roxanne is robbed on the bus en route to work and breaks into tears. She has nothing anyway, so why would someone want to rob her? Apologizing for their last date, which was a disaster, Dave Meyer shows up at McKenzie-Brackman and offers to lend Roxanne one of his cars until she's out of debt. Although reluctant to do so, she finally agrees and on her first day at work with a Mercedes, she finds a dozen roses on her desk. She goes to lunch with David and he tells her he's going away on business for a while and would like her to house-sit for him. Roxanne feels he's offering her charity, but he points out that she would actually be doing him a big favor. This she accepts too, while emphasizing that she can't offer him anything more than friendship. David eagerly accepts this.

McKenzie represents Vernon Kepler, who is involved in yet another assault charge. During preliminary meetings, Kepler brings his granddaughter Jennifer, a third year law student, with him. She plays an important role in convincing Kepler to offer a settlement. Unfortunately the victim, Steve Henderson, refuses to settle the issue. During the trial, we learn that Kepler struck him with his artificial leg after being called a thief. Opposing counsel Neil Robertson makes the point that the altercation came about because Kepler had lost a game of cribbage.

McKenzie all but gives up when, during cross-examination, an angry Kepler removes his leg and strikes Henderson with it yet again, this time in front of everyone. Robertson wants the leg held as evidence, which is laughed off by the judge. McKenzie plans on seeking no damages for anyone, which Kepler doesn't agree to until Jennifer talks him in to it. The jury comes back with no damages for either party, just as McKenzie had hoped. Impressed with Jennifer, Leland offers her a clerkship position at the firm, but she would much rather pursue a romantic relationship with him.

Van Owen is attempting to prosecute James Ray Edwards, who is charged with shooting security guard Walter Briles over some stolen jewelry. Her first witness is Julia Clarent. Under the cross-examination of black attorney Lee Atkins, Clarent admits that employees of the store initially were suspicious of Edwards because he was black. Van Owen's next witness is Briles himself, now wheelchair bound, who details what happened. Atkins again turns things around, implying that Briles provoked the attack because Edwards was black. Edwards is brought to the stand to testify. Van Owen objects and Atkins, yet again, turns everything to a racial issue, telling the jury his opponent is over-zealous because she was once shot by a black gang member and would like nothing more than to see Edwards put away.

The verdict: James Edwards is found not guilty. Van Owen's argument is that he was found not guilty for all the wrong reasons. That verdict was given because Atkins created an issue out of something that wasn't even an issue in the first place, and he persuaded the jury with it. Kuzak chalks it up to a legal strategy, and Van Owen claims she'll beat him next time.

(NOTE: The always incredible James Earl Jones portrays attorney Lee Atkins and makes a tremendous opponent for Grace Van Owen to come up against. Jones, of course, can be seen weekly on ABC's Gabriel's Fire, *supplied the voice of Darth Vader in George Lucas'* Star Wars *trilogy and most recently appeared on film in* Field of Dreams *and* The Hunt for Red October. *Dan O'Herlihy (Vernon Kepler) is probably best known to modern film audiences as "The Old Man" in* Robocop *and* Robocop 2.

SEASON THREE

PRODUCTION STAFF

Executive Producer: Steven Bochco
Co-Executive Producer: Rick Wallace
Supervising Producer: David E. Kelley
Producer: Scott Goldstein
Producer: Michelle Gallery
Coordinating Producer: Phillip Goldfarb
Coordinating Producer: Alice West

REGULAR CAST

Harry Hamlin: Michael Kuzak
Susan Dey: Grace Van Owen
Corbin Bernsen: Arnold Becker
Jill Eikenberry: Ann Kelsey
Alan Rachins: Douglas Brackman, Jr.
Michele Greene: Abby Perkins
Jimmy Smits: Victor Sifuentes
Michael Tucker: Stuart Markowitz
Susan Ruttan: Roxanne Melman
Richard Dysart: Leland McKenzie
Blair Underwood: Jonathan Rollins
Larry Drake: Benny Stulwicz

Episode Forty-Three

"Hey, Lick Me Over"

Written by Steven Bochco & David E. Kelley

Directed by Rick Wallace

Guest Stars: Dann Florek (David Meyer), Dana Sparks (Jennifer Kepler), Joe Spano (George Ripley), Alan Oppenheimer (Judge Stephen Weeks), David Neidorf (Gary Maus), Stanley Grover (Judge Richard Lobel), Matt McKenzie (Peter Montal), Gwen E. Davis (Voting Official), Janet Carroll (Judge Geraldine Parker), Stephen Anthony Henry (Jury Foreman), Coleen Maloney (Lisa Stewart), Lory Walsh (Marcia Jennings), Dan Hedaya (Michael Roitman), Herb Mitchell (Nicholas Patsos)

Van Owen's first case in the third season is a rather humorous one. George Ripley is charged with sticking his tongue in the ear of Lisa Stewart in a movie theater, supposedly because he simply couldn't help himself. Van Owen puts Ripley on the stand and questions him about other women he has licked without permission. After questioning, he starts to walk back to his seat and kisses Van Owen en route. This is enough to find Ripley guilty, although Van Owen, feeling sorry for him, agrees to one year probation accompanied by psychiatric care. In an elevator with Van Owen, Kuzak and a beautiful blonde woman, Ripley can't help himself and starts kissing the woman.

While Kuzak lobbies for Benny's right to vote in the upcoming election, Dave Meyer continues his efforts to romance Roxanne. She comes in one morning and tells Arnie that Dave proposed to her, but it's Becker's opinion she should marry for love, not money. Roxanne tells Dave she doesn't love him, but he says that doesn't matter. He's looking for companionship, and maybe, just maybe, the love will come lat-

er. With this in mind, she says yes to his proposal. On a Monday morning, Becker is really angry to find out that Rox got married without telling anyone. McKenzie plans an office party for them, and invites Jennifer along as his date.

The associates' reviews come in, with Sifuentes coming out on top, Rollins scoring quite well and the general consensus being that Abby is going to have to work harder if she wants to become a partner some day. Upon hearing this news, Abby becomes extremely defensive and talks about quitting the firm.

Sifuentes, who really does seem to get the most gut-wrenching cases, is representing Alex and Marcia Jennings—victims of a violent crime when an alarm company didn't respond to their call for help. While on the stand, Alex details how he pushed a silent alarm at his home prior to the brutal rape of his wife, a gun being placed to his head and their daughter being forced to watch the whole thing. Marcia is brought up to the stand next. Opposing counsel puts security company CEO Nicholas Patsos on the stand, and the man explains that the reason his security officers didn't enter the home was because the burglars were armed. This leads Sifuentes to attack company policy.

Security officer Gary Maus takes the stand and says he had only two weeks of training for the job. This goes directly against the company advertising which influenced the Jennings' decision to go with them. The next day, Sifuentes informs the Jennings of a fair settlement offer by the security company, but the family wants a public verdict. Thankfully they waited, as the jury finds Nicholas Patsos' company guilty and awards the Jennings a multi-million dollar verdict.

Episode Forty-Four

"The Son Also Rises"

Written by David E. Kelley

Directed by John Pasquin

Guest Stars: Rene Auberjonois (Mr. Richardson), Remy Auberjonois (Matthew Richardson), Gregg Henry (Robert Cullen), Bruce Kirby (D.A. Rogoff), Miriam Flynn (Madeline Meyer), Glenn Plummer (Lyle Torrey), Nicholas Mele (Robert Clark), Don Stewart (Mitchell Nelson), Michael Laskin (Judge London), Ken Lerner (Peter Duble), James Avery (Judge Michael Conover), Peter Neptune (Freddy), Nick Eldredge (Scott Reynolds), Tommy Hollis (Geoffrey Marchant), Karen Hensel (Mrs. Chesbro), Mary Armstrong (Jury Foreperson), Laura Drake (Mrs. Richardson), Dana Sparks (Jennifer Kepler), Dann Florek (David Meyer), Dave Florek (Policeman)

Despite McKenzie's reasoning to the contrary, Abby sticks to her guns about quitting McKenzie-Brackman. She is going to open her own business. Leland can appreciate this and offers any support he can, including the resources of the firm. Abby thanks him.

Kelsey represents 13-year-old Matthew Richardson, who is suing his father for slapping him. The boy offers to settle if his father will apologize, but the man, Kevin, will not. A screaming match between the Richardsons and their attorneys develops and Markowitz intervenes with a speech about fathers and sons. His words are particularly emotional, undoubtedly based on the fact that he and Kelsey have thus far been unable to conceive a child. This little talk seems to have the desired effect, as father and son work out their differences, lay down some ground rules and are united again.

Roxanne talks Becker into helping her sister-in-law Madeline, who is breaking up with husband Freddy. The two of them meet with Dave and Madeline, and she rambles on about her business in the same way that Dave does about his. Apparently it runs in the family. Becker gives Roxanne a restraining order to keep Freddy away from Madeline, but when he gets in his office he finds the woman's dog, which needs a home for a few days while her house is being done over. At first Becker is furious about being taken advantage of, but he eventually finds himself attached to the dog (Oliver).

Arnie's problems with this particular case never seem to end, as Roxanne runs into his office stating that Freddy is bulldozing the house. Arnie races over with Oliver in the front seat of his Porsche, and he arrives just as the police do. The officers won't stop Freddy because he has a permit to do what he's doing, but Becker points out that the bulldozer isn't registered. Seeing that this is true, the police stop Freddy with only a portion of the house demolished. Freddy is ordered to back up, and he does so—right over Becker's car and, apparently, Oliver. Happily, the dog lives.

Van Owen and District Attorney Bruce Rogoff avoid the press regarding their case against Lyle Torrey, who is accused of killing two police officers. Their chief witness is Irene Chesbro, but Torrey's lawyer, Robert Cullen, puts some doubt in her mind. Van Owen's next witness is Geoffrey Merchant, who heard Torrey brag about the killings while they were in jail. Cullen's response is to emphasize that Merchant is a felon and well-known liar. Torrey is brought up to the stand next, where he is cross-examined by both attorneys.

During a recess, Merchant's attorney asks Van Owen about the deal that was struck for his client to get Torrey to confess while in jail. Van Owen doesn't know what the man is talking about, and heads into Rogoff's office,

Susan Ruttan portrays legal secretary Roxanne Melman.

Harry Hamlin portrays Michael Kuzak.

threatening to throw the case out. Rogoff, who is well aware of Grace's feelings about the law, asks her to ignore the circumstances this one time. She has to think about the public, not the individual. *Very* reluctantly she agrees, and delivers her closing argument, as does Cullen. Torrey is found guilty of murder, but Van Owen has no joy.

Episode Forty-Five

"Romancing the Drone"

Written by William M. Finkelstein

Directed by Win Phelps

Guest Stars: Debra Sandlund (Jane Lauderbach), Jennifer Bassey (Judge Caplan), Kevin Gage (Calvin Sholes), Peter Hansen (Judge Jeffrey Liddle), Bruce Kirby (D.A. Rogoff), Dann Florek (David Meyer), Paul Miceli-Sanchez (William Plank), Elizabeth North (Rosalind), James Oden Hatch (Howard), Joann Linville (Rona Samuels), John Bennett Perry (Richard Lauderbach), Pamela Reed (Norma Heisler), Claudette Nevins (Sarah Schindler), Walter Addison (Dr. Klein), Emily K. Kuroda (Ronnie), Cynthia Sikes (Judge Monica Ryan)

Dr. Klein, an infertility specialist, asks Markowitz for a sperm sample, after Stuart learns the problem with conceiving a child does not lay with Kelsey. His sperm count is low, which is completely depressing to him.

Abby sets up shop and prosecutor Jim Aoli works it out for her to represent alleged robber William Plank. Sifuentes and Rollins visit her office to congratulate her.

Dave Meyer makes Roxanne late for work due to his forcing her to listen to his new cassette sales pitch. He comes to McKenzie-Brackman during the day to apologize to her, and delivers a sales spiel to Becker, which embarrasses Roxanne and she verbally lets him

have it. She talks to Arnie about how embarrassed she is, and his response is to criticize her for the way she treated her husband. When Dave gets home that night, Roxanne greets him at the door with a drink in her hand and his cassette sales pitch playing over the stereo system. Dave hugs her, overjoyed at the way she's willing to participate in his life.

Becker is representing Jane Lauderbach, whose husband has a tendency to set her up with other men so he could watch them make love. He goes to Judge Liddle in regard to her suit for emotional distress, but opposing counsel Rona Samuels argues that there is already a no-fault divorce settlement in place. Liddle nonetheless allows for limited discovery. Becker and Jane eventually meet with her husband, Richard, and the man's attorney to discuss the couple's sexual activities. In this conversation, it's revealed that Jane took drugs to unlock her inhibitions. Despite Becker's arguments to the contrary, Jane decides to drop her suit against Richard.

Kuzak is involved in a pro bono case, this one in defense of accused rapist Calvin Sholes, who discusses victim Norma Heisler in such a way that it's actually repulsive. On the witness stand, Norma details how Sholes raped her repeatedly on the kitchen floor. She adds that he had been reading her private diary before the incident occurred, and Kuzak demands the diary be made a part of the court's record. Judge Caplan has no choice but to order her to bring it in the following day.

When the book is brought in, Kuzak reads the entries which deal with fantasies Norma wrote regarding Sholes. She tries to dismiss these as her private thoughts, not an invitation to be raped. The jury finds Sholes guilty, which pleases Kuzak no end. He offers his apologies to Norma, but she essentially tells him to go to hell. Later, Kuzak and Van Owen get into a serious argument over their respective views of the lawyer in society.

As often happens when Becker gets too close to someone, he starts trying to distance himself. The cycle repeats itself with Monica as he attacks her for everything she says, plays the poor martyr and the couple breaks up.

(NOTE: Pamela Reed (Norma Heisler) has most recently been seen in NBC's now-defunct series Grand, *and the Arnold Schwarzenegger film* Kindergarten Cop.)

Episode Forty-Six

"Sperminator"

Written by Michele Gallery

Directed by Tom Moore

Guest Stars: Wayne Northrop (Bill Ringstrom), Troy Evans (Nathaniel Holland), Deborah May (Carla Stritch), Lisa Sutton (Maura Coyle), Madison Mason (Peter Osteen), Michael Pniewski (Judge McCall), Frances E. Nealey (Juror), Ellen Blake (Elizabeth Brand), Martin Azarow (Robert Sylvia), Emily K. Kuroda (Ronnie), Gregg Berger (Mitchell Noyes), Ken Foree (Leonard Mosher), Abraham Alvarez (Judge Blanke), Ralph Bruneau (Frank Swayze), Nana Visitor (Betsy Major)

Rollins is given a wrongful death case, but is angered when Sifuentes (despite his own objections) is assigned to act as second counsel. The case is Coyle vs. Terra Nova Instruments. Laura Coyle filed a suit against the company because the company's CEO told her husband to go on a mountain climbing trip or be passed over for promotion. A tragic accident occurred and the man plummeted to his death.

Thinking he's doing the right thing, though he couldn't be farther from the truth, Rollins shows Mrs. Coyle a photo of her husband's smashed and bloody remains immediately following the fall, sending the woman into hysterics. Opposing counsel takes advantage of this moment, making Rollins look like a monster. Sifuentes receives permission from the judge to ask questions of the witness, and establishes the importance of this little excursion into nature in order to secure a promotion. Rollins is angry at Sifuentes for doing this, but Victor believes it's the only thing that's going to get the jury back on their side.

By the end of the trial, Sifuentes gives Rollins the opportunity to deliver the closing argument and essentially redeem himself. Now filled with humility rather than confidence, Rollins appeals to the jury to forget about his earlier stunt and focus on the issue at hand. The jury finds in favor of Mrs. Coyle, with one of the jurists telling Rollins that a little humble pie is good once in a while.

Because of all the arguing they've been doing as of late, Kuzak refuses to take Van Owen's phone calls. Eventually, though, they do get together and Grace tells him she's been so distant because she compromised herself in the Lyle Torrey case.

As Abby begins her career as an individual lawyer, Becker sets up a free consultation for her with his publicist and it goes tremendously well. Brackman refers Whitey Holland to Abby for representation, although she has only one day to prepare for his court date. She tries for a continuance but is turned down by the judge, for she is the third lawyer Holland has brought in with him and this is the third request for a continuance. Shocked, Abby tells Holland that she won't represent him because he lied to her.

That night, Holland comes by her office to apologize and begs her to take his case. Abby refuses and he becomes violent, coming at her with a metal pipe, threatening to kill her. Abby grabs her purse, pulls out a pistol and empties it into his body. Holland collapses to the ground lifelessly. The police arrive and Lieutenant Bill Ringstrom gives Abby her cover story—that the gun was in her desk for self protection and she had to use it. If not, she would be in trouble for walking around with a weapon. Abby heads home to get a message from her publicist on the answering machine. The woman says they'll turn this tragedy into a positive. Abby laughs and cries at the same time.

Episode Forty-Seven

"Princess and the Pee"

Written by William M. Finkelstein

Directed by Sam Weisman

Guest Stars: Nancy Vawter (Dorothy Wyler), Tracy Burns (Ms. Simon), Wayne Northrop (Bill Ringstrom), Michael Fairman (Judge McGrath), Kurt Fuller (Stan Nausbaum), David Spielberg (Judge Reeves), Joanna Frank (Sheila Brackman), Emily Kuroda (Ronnie), Brad Jeffries (Randy Huggins), Randolph Mantooth (Gil Tecowsky), Charles Young (Jeff), Mitchell Laurance (Richard Mathers), Ron Leath (Barry Toland), Rosemary Dunsmore (Ina Toland), Anne Marie Gillis (Dr. Wagner)

Brackman's divorce settlement is going along fine, until he learns that Sheila doesn't want to share a burial plot with him. In fact, she wants to totally disassociate herself with him, right down to taking back her maiden name, Slutsky. After hiring 52-year-old Dorothy Wyler, a divorcee, as an associate, Brackman learns that life can indeed go on after divorce. This is the moment that makes him realize he doesn't have to hold on to Sheila in any way. He tells her he's dropping the dual-plot

idea, so a settlement can be filed immediately.

Kelsey and Markowitz try everything possible for her to become pregnant. As one method after another fails, they consider the idea of adoption as a means of starting a family.

While trying to cope with the fact that she killed someone in self defense, Abby attempts to balance her rapidly growing case load. To get a handle on things, she asks Van Owen to help her get a continuance in the case of Val Necco, a drug dealer. Although she doesn't like the idea, Grace agrees to it, despite an admonishing she has to take from the judge.

Later, Lieutenant Ringstrom arrives at Abby's office with the signed testimony of a necessary witness who previously refused to testify. Frustrated that she has to depend so much on other people to get her job done, Abby breaks down in tears. Ringstrom tries to comfort her by sharing his similar feeling of everything becoming overwhelming after he had killed someone in the line of duty. He adds that he's feeling an attraction to her and Abby, despite herself, admits to the same thing.

Before Wyler is hired, Kuzak suggests they consider Richard Mathers, who he's currently up against in court, as an associate. Rollins does some research on Mathers and is shocked to learn that the man isn't really a lawyer. Armed with this information, Kuzak confronts the man and suggests that they accept the settlement offer in the Tecowsky case. Mathers will not, stating that he will fight on and it's up to Kuzak to decide whether or not he'll turn him in. The trial ends in favor of Kuzak's client, but Mathers calls for a mistrial, noting that he is not a lawyer and that Kuzak was well aware of the fact. The judge is angry over this, and tells Kuzak that he will face disciplinary actions from the bar association.

Episode Forty-Eight

"Dummy Dearest"

Written by Robert Cochran

Directed by Ben Holt

Guest Stars: Mitchell Laurance (Richard Mathers), Ronn Lucas (Kenny Peterson), Jennifer Rhodes (D.A. Gylkowski), Al Fann (Judge Syler), Nancy Vawter (Dorothy Wyler), Charlie Stratton (Michael Lyons), Gerald Anthony (Ross Burnett), Greg Rusin (Ralph Bellini), Michael P. Keenan (Dr. Shale), Jack R. Orend (Judge Adelstein), Fred E. Baker (Carl Nelson), Mort Sertner (Judge Donald Tytell), Darlene Kardon (Judge Constance Gregg), George Coe (Judge Vance), Jerry Hauck (Elliot Oppenheim), D. Paul Thomas (Ralph De-Suvio), Jennifer Darling (Amanda Shaw), Joel Brooks (Kiefir Mitchell), Dann Florek (David Meyer), Ron Perkins (D.A. Lemoyne), John Michael Bolger (Officer Jordan)

Benny finds himself fascinated with Kenny Peterson, a ventriloquist, and his dummy, Gilbert. Things are less than amusing, however, when the dummy starts to insult him. Rollins has been given Peterson's case. The man is charged with assault and resisting arrest, but will speak only through Gilbert, and every word out of Gilbert's mouth is cruel. During the first day in court, Rollins is trying to deliver his opening statements when Gilbert starts screaming out interruptions. The judge gives Rollins one more day to get his "team" in order.

The following day, Kenny's psychiatrist is put on the stand and he explains that due to a childhood trauma the man will speak only through Gilbert. Once again Gilbert starts his insults, though this time they're directed to the judge. The case is postponed for one year provided that Kenny resumes

psychiatric care. After that time, a decision will be made. Later, Benny overhears Gilbert yelling at Kenny, calling him a wimp and so on.

Benny steps into the room and tells Gilbert off, noting that the reason Gilbert doesn't want Kenny to speak is that if he did, Gilbert would not be needed. Although it's a major effort, Kenny speaks in his own voice and thanks Benny for sticking up for him. Benny, a retarded man working in a law firm, is inspiration enough for him to deal with his situation.

Richard Mathers tells Kuzak he'll speak positively of him during Michael's hearing if Kuzak will do the same for him, but Michael refuses. Mathers has no choice but to subpoena Kuzak to testify in his behalf. Sifuentes represents Kuzak before the State Bar Disciplinary Committee, but they really don't take any pity on him. They rule Kuzak cannot practice law for one month. To make matters worse, McKenzie doesn't want him to come to the office while he's under suspension, fearing the image it might portray.

Kelsey and Markowitz meet with adoption attorney Ross Burnett to discuss the idea of getting a child. Burnett emphasizes that even though they're lawyers, they are going to have to drop whatever they're doing when contacted by a birth mother.

Kelsey represents Amanda Shaw in her suit against the *National Informer*, which reported that the woman allegedly had an affair with her daughter's boyfriend. This libelous story resulted in the girl killing herself. Now Amanda is suing for damages. Kelsey calls the girl's boyfriend, Michael Lyons to the stand, and he testifies that the newspaper never contacted him to try and verify the story. The *Informer* attorney, Kiefir Mitchell, calls reporter Ralph Bellini to the stand, and he clouds thing even more with testimony about a rumor that Amanda Shaw had an abortion as a result of the affair. The jury finds in favor of Shaw, but the next day the front page of the *National Informer* screams, "Amanda Aborts Teen Love Child?" Due to the fact the issue was brought up during the trial, the paper has a legal right to print the story.

(NOTE: Gerald Anthony (Ross Burnett) was a regular on the soap opera One Life to Live *and on* Wiseguy.*)*

Episode Forty-Nine

"To Live and Diet in L.A."

Written by Judith Parker

Directed by John Pasquin

Guest Stars: Gregg Henry (Robert Cullen), Bruce Kirby (D.A. Rogoff), Glenn Plummer (Lyle Torrey), Nancy Vawter (Dorothy Wyler), Gerald Anthony (Ross Burnett), Wayne Northrop (Bill Ringstrom), James Avery (Judge Michael Conover), Stan Kamber (Judge Shubow), Charles Fulcher (Clerk), Mary Tanner (Kelly), Mary Armstrong (Foreperson), Darlene Harris (Juror Falder), Bernie Casey (Lt. Dolan), Joyce Hyser (Allison Gottlieb), Marco Hernandez (Jose Higuel), Jon C. Slade (Thomas Griese), Harold Ayer (Dean Paige), Ernie Fuentes (Juror Douse), Jill Vance (Secretary), Jimi Bridges, Jr. (Suspect), Harry Hart-Browne (Waiter), Terry Israel (Clerk), Lorna Scott (Juror Bennett), Dr. Bernie Ernst (Dale), Jeanne Ernst (Margo), Kim Murdock (Reporter #2), Robert Pescovitz (Reporter #1)

Abby and Ringstrom's attraction for each other grows more intense and when Ringstrom takes her to a hotel restaurant for lunch, he expresses a desire to sleep with her. Abby, charmed by his sense of confidence in having them eat at this location, agrees and they head upstairs to a room.

Kelsey and Markowitz meet with young Kelly for lunch and they discuss each other's background. By the end of lunch, Kelly is convinced that they would be good parents to her unborn child. Afterward, the couple begins making plans for the baby. Unfortunately, Kelly changes her mind later on and Burnett suggests that her parents may have convinced her to let a friend's family adopt the child. Markowitz is like a rock, encouraging Kelsey, stating that some day they will be united with the soul of their baby. Markowitz heads to the men's room, where he breaks down and cries.

Dave Meyer buys into the distribution of a video diet tape, which Roxanne begins to follow in an effort to lose weight. Becker comes into the office while the couple is watching the tape, and he expresses his fascination for "lifestyle" programming. Meyer considers this for a moment, and suggests that there would be some serious money to be made in a do-it-yourself-divorce tape. The idea intrigues Becker's imagination. They work out a deal and Meyer brings a camera crew into the office. Director Allison Gottlieb works it out in such a way that Becker's natural charm and charisma comes through on tape. Later, Meyer brings a life-size standing photo of Becker to the office, explaining that it will be used as a point-of-purchase display for the video. Becker, who has no problem in the ego department, likes the image.

Van Owen is horrified to learn that Lyle Torrey is going to die by way of lethal gas. Since she knows that the man's confession was illegally obtained, she recognizes the ramifications of misusing the system. Van Owen insists on the case being reopened. In response, Lieutenant Dolan "accidentally" misses a court appearance where Van Owen is representing the D.A., causing the case to be thrown out by the judge. Later, Detective Ringstrom (Abby's "friend") informs Grace that there will be no help coming from the police department if she gets a cop killer back on the streets.

After asking Judge Conover if he'll repress an internal investigation, Van Owen works out a deal with Dolan and Torrey's attorney. Torrey will identify the suspects in a series of drive-by shootings, and for that he will be set free. Dolan doesn't like it, but he ultimately agrees to the idea. The deal is put into motion, but it isn't long before Torrey is killed on the streets in a gang-like shooting. Van Owen comes to the scene and accuses Dolan of killing him. Dolan unconvincingly claims that neither he or his men had anything to do with it.

(NOTE: Character actor Bernie Casey (Lieutenant Dolan) has appeared in such films as the James Bond thriller Never Say Never Again, I'm Gonna Git You Sucker *and* Another 48 Hrs.*)*

Episode Fifty

"I'm in the Nude For Love"

Written by David E. Kelley

Directed by Eric Laneuville

Guest Stars: Joyce Hyser (Allison Gottlieb), Niles Brewster (Upton Weeks), Robert Ellenstein (Dr. Lacker), Micole Mercurio (Mrs. Ferguson), Dennis Bailey (Dick), Ron Orbach (Charles Knotts), Michael Laskin (Judge London), Nancy Vawter (Dorothy Wyler), Dale Swann (Dr. Allard), Richie Allan (Mr. Ferguson), Charles Hoyes (Bartender), Alicia O'Connor (Jamie Ferguson), Teri Hatcher (Tracy Shoe), Noble Willingham (Robert Kenyon), Allan Arbus (Lawrence Stone), Macon McCalman (Judge Baldwin)

Kelsey represents Lawrence Stone's nudist colony, which has been slapped with a nuisance complaint from the surrounding neighbors. To get more information, Kuzak asks to speak to Tra-cy Shoe, winner of the Miss Nude Galaxy contest, and she walks in naked. Tracy is put on the stand and actually works against the colony by mentioning that she *may* have had sexual feelings toward some of the local boys who would sneak on to the property. Realizing that this is probably the end of his colony, Stone asks Kuzak to get him some time so that he can sell the property before a decision is made.

On further investigation, Kuzak realizes that there are several real estate companies after the colony's property, but he is shocked to learn that the company that wants it the most has Tracy as a partner. She purposely tried to destroy Stone's case. Kuzak confronts her, telling Tracy that he will hold up the sale on the grounds of fraud unless she and her partners up the offer by half a million dollars. She has no choice but to accept the deal. Kuzak and Van Owen attend a "going out of business" party for the colony, and Grace shocks him by removing her clothes. After all, when in Rome. . . .

(NOTE: The hints of nudity in this episode are quite startling, and not quite what one would expect from a network television show.)

While Benny and Allison Gottlieb await the arrival of Becker at a bar, one of the patrons starts hitting on Allison in a not-so-polite way. Benny grows angry, hoists the guy off the ground and demands an apology. In a show of appreciation, Allison sends Benny some flowers and he instantly develops a crush on her. He gets angry, though, when he sees Becker kiss her hand later on, and is convinced they're only his friend because they feel sorry for him. They assure him it isn't true, but Benny will have to work it out for himself. Eventually he apologizes to Becker.

Sifuentes is representing a hospital that doesn't want to turn off the life support system of Jamie Ferguson, despite her parents' wish that they do so. The argument is that she is not brain dead and is therefore only depending on the machinery for nutrients. Mr. and Mrs. Ferguson beg Judge Baldwin to allow their daughter to die in dignity, but Sifuentes counters that by asking the hospital to shut off the machines keeping her alive, they want to starve Jamie to death. The doctors explain that there is a possibility Jamie could make a recovery, and Sifuentes' only recourse is to ask that Jamie be brought in.

The next day, Jamie is brought in, the only part of her body moving being her eyes, which float sporadically. The Fergusons break down in tears, and Sifuentes isn't that far from them himself. Judge Baldwin takes the case under advisement and comes back with the decision that he must preserve the sanctity of life. The machines shall remain on. After the court session ends, Mr. Ferguson criticizes Sifuentes for making their hell go on even longer. Alone in the elevator, Sifuentes collapses, not liking himself very much.

Episode Fifty-One

"Victor Victorious"

Written by David E. Kelley, Michele Gallery and Judith Parker

Directed by Win Phelps

Guest Stars: James Earl Jones (Lee Atkins), Joyce Hyser (Allison Gottlieb), Art Hindle (Walter Goetz), Nancy Vawter (Dorothy Wyler), Mike Genovese (Charles Bassett), Gerald Anthony (Ross Burnett), Emily Kuroda (Ronnie), Teddy Wilson (Jerome Seely), Tzi Ma (Mark Milley), Anne Haney (Judge Travelini)

Although Allison rejects Becker's advances for a date, Sifuentes nonetheless tries to give it a shot and surprisingly, she says yes. They hit it off instantly and engage in a passionate affair.

Abby is having financial difficulties in her own practice and starts to short-change clients by accepting lower than necessary settlements. Learning about this, Markowitz tells Abby she seems to be looking out more for her own best interests than those of her clients. Abby doesn't take well to the criticism, but later apologizes, saying he's probably right. Understanding the pressure she's under, Markowitz sets her up with a high-paying client.

Markowitz and Kelsey are contacted by Ross Burnett, who says there is a plane arriving with a baby on board if they want it. But they must make the decision immediately. They head to the airport and Kelsey starts to get the jitters, until she actually looks at the baby and holds it in her arms. Maternal instincts take over, a dream apparently has come true and the new Markowitz family heads for home.

Van Owen is pitted against her old foe Lee Atkins, who is representing Jerome Seely, alleged murderer of an intruder he shot in the back. She checks into Seely's background and determines that the man is guilty. Seeing he could very well lose this case, Atkins tries to get a mistrial declared, claiming that his client has accused him of misrepresentation. Van Owen tells the judge that Atkins has a history of being sued by his clients when it looks as though he's going to lose a case.

The trial continues and Atkins delivers his closing argument, emphasizing that racial prejudice is what influenced his client's actions. Atkins cites statistics to validate his point and Van Owen responds by saying Atkins is trying to introduce new evidence. It results in Atkins himself being put on the witness stand, where Van Owen really lashes into him, tearing apart his character. Stunningly, the judge declares a mistrial because Van Owen's argument has been so strong, there's no way Seely could get a fair trial. Afterwards, Atkins smiles at Grace and she realizes she fell right into his game of manipulation.

(NOTE: James Earl Jones returns as Atkins and is just as terrific as he was the previous season. If not for his own series, Gabriel's Fire, *one would assume that he might have come back to the folds of* L.A. Law.*)*

Episode Fifty-Two

"The Plane Mutiny"

Written by Sandy Smolan, Steven Bochco, David E. Kelley and William M. Finkelstein

Directed by Sandy Smolan

Guest Stars: Kathleen Lloyd (Adrian Joyner), Dann Florek (Dave Meyer), Christina Belford (Lily White), Stan Kamber (Judge Shubow), Graham Beckel (Willie Kosar), Michele Pawk (Astrid), Michael Durrell (Joseph Schaeffer), Michael David Lally (John Dunham), Ami Rothschild (Odette), Alec Murdock (Reporter #1), Kim Murdock (Reporter #2), Dante di Loretto (D.A. Robert Appel), Nancy Vawter (Dorothy Wyler), Mike Muscat (Bessen), Nigel Gibbs (Passenger #1), Lindsay Frost (Stephanie Hall), Donald Hotton (Passenger #2), Ken Letner (Captain Laughlin), Michele Harrell (Judy), Gene Borkan (Top Shirt), Stuart Nisbet (Grant), Rose Weaver (Judge Keresy), Philip Sterling (Judge Cramer)

Dave Meyer tells Becker that the royalties for their video should be quite high, which fills him with joy. That joy dissipates, however, when Brackman brings up a clause in the man's contract which says that a percentage of any earnings he makes as a lawyer must be given to the partners. Not liking the idea too much, Becker turns to his own attorney. This does no good as she tells Becker that the partners are entitled to 5/6 of his royalties. Becker offers to make the split 75-25, but it ends up 50-50.

Brackman is on a plane to Chicago, which stops indefinitely on the runway before taking off. He insists on being taken back to the terminal for fear of losing what could be a major client, but the captain refuses. Brackman uses another passenger's cellular telephone and gets Rollins to get a court order for the plane to pull back to the terminal. Once they get there, the captain has him arrested for interfering with a normal flight and for using a cellular phone on an airplane. In court, Brackman handles himself perfectly, arguing his point in such a way that the judge dismisses all charges. Ironically the woman he borrowed the cellular phone from also is a lawyer and was en route to see the same client. Brackman asks her out to dinner and she accepts. Things work out nicely, though, because the company in Chicago is so impressed with the way he beat the airline that it wants McKenzie-Brackman to handle its legal affairs. Finally, Douglas comes out the good guy and scores a big one!

Sifuentes is pit against Van Owen in court. He represents Joseph Schaeffer, accused of hiring a hit man to kill his wife. What Sifuentes wants to do is locate middle man Willie Kosar, who arranged for the actual hit. The judge refuses to give him the extra time he needs, so he hires a private investigator named Stephie Hall. The reason he is so desperate to find Kosar is that Schaeffer allegedly was intoxicated when he said he wanted his wife dead, but tried to call it off once he sobered up. Becker is put on the stand to testify as a character witness to Schaeffer, but Van Owen easily is able to destroy his credibility as a judge of character.

At the last minute, Sifuentes learns that Hall has located Kosar. Sifuentes goes to Kosar's hotel room, demanding that he tell the court that Schaeffer tried to call the hit off. Kosar refuses, until Hall says she has enough evidence to get the man himself convicted. Kosar goes on the stand and testifies that Schaeffer did indeed try to call the hit off. Van Owen offers a settlement of one year suspended provided Schaeffer enter a plea of conspiracy to commit assault. That is an acceptable deal and the trial comes to a close.

Later, in the parking garage, Van Owen compliments Sifuentes' abilities as a lawyer and kisses him, stating that's something she's wanted to do for a long time—and something that she won't be doing again.

Episode Fifty-Three

"Izzy Ackerman, Or Is He Not?"

Written by Joe Shulkin, Dan Benzvi and William M. Finkelstein

Directed by Sam Weisman

Guest Stars: Michael Warren (Ray Davis), Phil Rubenstein (Nate Greenberg), Don Sparks (Russell Spitzer), Annie Abbott (Judge Neiman), Morgan Brittany (Tammy Jacobs), Eric Menyuk (Roland Burnet), Marilyn Ptizer (Liz), Fred Ponzlov (Clerk), Jay Arlen Jones (Cop #1), Suanne Spoke (Cop #2), Lesley Boone (Gretchen), Keith Mills (Judge Green), Nancy Vawter (Dorothy Wyler), Paul Collins (George Lindquist), Barry Braunstein (Kevin Dunn), Wayne Northrop (Bill Ringstrom), Mary Anne McGarry (Sarah Halpern), Lloyd Gordon (William Riley), Jack Bruskoff (Milton), Herb Muller (Fat Morty), David Gale (Marvin Fitzgerald)

At a weight loss center, one of the women criticizes Roxanne's rotten sex life as being a result of her weight, and Rox punches the woman out. Next day she's arrested for battery. Becker and Roxanne meet with the woman, Tammy, and her lawyer. Tammy wants Rox to pay for a nose, chin and eye job, as well as liposuction and a week at a resort. To make matters worse, her life with Dave Meyer is completely depressing her and Arnie suggests she see a marriage counsellor. She and Meyer do so and Roxanne lets loose with all the fury that's been building up inside of her. The reason she is so unhappy is that she doesn't love him and never has!

(NOTE: Dann Florek is such a great mope as Dave Meyer, that you have to feel sorry for the poor schlep, and are kind of forced to get angry at the way Roxanne treats him.)

A mix-up in corpses has Izzy Ackerman's body mistaken for one of an organ donor, and various body parts are shipped to different locations. McKenzie sets upon getting all of the man's parts back in one location. All of them except the man's head are returned, with McKenzie declaring, "Bring me the head of Izzy Ackerman!" Leland threatens to sue the company responsible for the mix-up. The head is finally returned in an ice chest and a procession of people head out of McKenzie's office. Benny accidentally bumps into Izzy's cousin Morty, and the man drops the ice chest, causing Izzy's head to roll across the floor. Certainly a dark and rather sick story line that Stephen King would no doubt enjoy.

Kuzak represents Ray Davis, who is suing a hospital that allegedly let his wife die because they didn't have insurance. Davis asks him to have an open mind to a settlement offer, and insists that he be allowed to take the stand at some point. After Dr. McKenna takes the stand and his testimony is incriminating, the hospital offers $300,000. Ray and Kuzak decide they will push on. As the trial continues, opposing counsel presents documents which prove that Mrs. Davis was not legally divorced from her previous husband when she married Ray. The judge, realizing that the Davis' weren't married, throws the case out of court. Kuzak is furious at himself for not having discovered this and Brackman is nervous that they might be sued for malpractice. Let's face it, this has not been a good season for Michael Kuzak.

Kuzak and Van Owen eat a restaurant. On their way out, they bump into Detective Bill Ringstrom . . . and his wife.

Episode Fifty-Four

"The Accidental Jurist"

Written by Steven Bochco, David E. Kelley, Michele Gallery and Judith Parker

Directed by Jan Eliasberg

Guest Stars: Donald Moffat (Judge O'Neil), Dann Florek (David Meyer), Brian McNamara (Matthew Leonard), Alan Rosenberg (William Willis), Nancy Vawter (Dorothy Wyler), Wayne Northrop (Bill Ringstrom), Juleen Murray (Sally Ringstrom), Carol Barbee (Penelope), Emily Kuroda (Ronnie), Fae Rubenstein (Sally McMahon), Jack McGee (Brianson), Joyce Hyser (Allison Gottlieb), Elizabeth Hoffman (Jeanne Rubens), Michael Cavanaugh (Paul Richardson), Jack Rader (Sardo), Glenn Walker Harris, Jr. (Peter Ringstrom)

When Abby learns that Ringstrom is really married, she goes to his office to see him and really lets him have it. Ringstrom responds that he waited all along for Abby to ask personal questions about him, but she never did. Obviously she didn't want to know anything too personal about him. Abby is forced to accept this, though she refuses to see him any longer now that she knows the truth.

Kelsey fires the baby's nanny and is forced to bring the child to work with her. At the same time, she tries inter-viewing prospective nannies but her requirements are so tough she is unable to find anyone suitable. Throughout the day, she and Markowitz hand the baby to each other and the results are, to say the least chaotic.

Dave Meyer goes away on a business trip, and Roxanne confesses to Becker that she enjoys the quiet. She enjoys it so much, in fact, that when Dave comes home, she tells him she thinks they should separate for a while. Without putting up any kind of fight, Dave trudges off into the rainy night. The following day, the two of them go to their marriage counsellor and Dave explodes at Roxanne that she had better start appreciating him for who he is, or she can get out of the marriage. Next morning, he comes to McKenzie-Brackman and apologizes for the way he blew up. Roxanne actually liked him asserting himself, and asks him to come home.

Kuzak is representing Olympic champion Matthew Leonard, suing to keep a multi-million dollar endorsement contract despite the fact that he recently acknowledged his homosexuality in public. The sessions will be held in private and Kuzak does what he can to manipulate things so that they get Judge O'Neil, who also is gay—although that isn't public knowledge. American Food Corporation lawyer William Willis wants to know why Leonard waited so long to make his homosexuality public.

He admits he was afraid to, which makes Willis want to know why American Food also shouldn't be afraid. After hearing both sides, Judge O'Neil rules in favor of the corporation. Kuzak apologizes to Leonard, feeling that his thinking regarding a judge may have been off. In a private moment, O'Neil lets Kuzak know that he's well aware that the lawyer had him investigated and learned he's gay. In this case, notes O'Neill, a gay judge probably worked

Lawyer Abby Perkins, portrayed by Michele Greene.

Sometimes-sleazy divorce lawyer Arnie Becker, portrayed by Corbin Bernsen, makes periodic efforts to clean up his act.

against him.

Kuzak wants a mistrial or he'll appeal on the grounds of judicial bias. O'Neil refuses, despite the fact that Kuzak's appeal would let the world know he's a homosexual. Kuzak goes to Leonard with the idea, but, surprisingly, Leonard turns him down, feeling O'Neil has the right to keep his homosexuality private.

Episode Fifty-Five

"Barstow Bound"

Written by William M. Finkelstein

Directed by Win Phelps

Guest Stars: Dann Florek (David Meyer), Nancy Vawter (Dorothy Wyler), Harry Goaz (Arthur Simon), Andy Romano (Barney Dowe), John Goff (Pat Clausen), John Bedford Lloyd (Duane), Gary Sandy (Andrew Barnett), Nancy Paul (Hallie), Jim Antonio (Walter Olshan), Myra Turley (Mary Fitzpatrick), Kim Murdock (Reporter), Vince Melocchi (Murray Rosenfeld), J.J. Johnston (Roy Steinmetz), Mary Gregory (Judge Pendleton)

As everyone is well aware, Becker's "do-it-yourself-divorce" video is a great success. Unfortunately, many of the husbands across America don't appreciate the tape. One of them, Duane Butler, shows up in Becker's office, claiming that ever since his wife saw the tape, it's ruined his marriage. Becker suggests they get some counselling, but from Duane's angry look as he walks out of the office, we can see that's something he won't be looking into for quite some time. Trying to put this out of his mind, Becker goes with Dave Meyer to an autograph signing in a local bookstore and is shocked by the number of beautiful women who are there.

After the book signing, Becker walks to his car and is grabbed by Duane But-

ler, who is in a pickup. Raising a shotgun to Becker's face, he makes him climb in the truck and they head to his trailer home. Inside, Arnie finds himself facing Duane's wife, Hallie. Duane threatens to kill Arnie just to prove how much he loves Hallie. Hallie manages to talk the gun away from him. Breaking down, Duane leaves the trailer. Hallie takes off her clothes and asks Becker to take her away from this life. Disgusted, he leaves the trailer, realizing that stardom is not what it's cracked up to be.

Sifuentes represents Mary Fitzpatrick in a wrongful death claim against Steinmetz Construction. The argument is that Steinmetz bribed building inspectors to ignore the building codes, and a cement floor collapsed on Charlie Fitzpatrick because construction didn't meet standards. Sifuentes puts building inspector Walter Olshan on the stand, and he finally admits his orders were to look the other way. Added to this is the fact that Steinmetz promised Congressman Barnett the job would be done on time no matter what.

While this is going on, Leland has been asked by Arthur Simon to accept a nomination for a Federal Judgeship and Simon would like Sifuentes to back off the Steinmetz case. Next day at the office, McKenzie asks Sifuentes if he's ready to battle the political machine that is Congressman Barnett, to which he responds in the affirmative. This is enough for Leland, who does not pursue the issue any further.

In an attempt to clear his name, Barnett appears in court and takes the stand. During his examination, Sifuentes establishes the fact that Steinmetz contributed significantly to Barnett's last political campaign and that more recently he built a luxurious home for the congressman. This is enough for Judge Pendleton to give Sifuentes two additional weeks to go over Barnett's overall involvement with Steinmetz.

Like any politician, Barnett doesn't want negative publicity and tries to work out a settlement arrangement with Mary Fitzpatrick. Because she needs the money, she accepts the settlement. She is convinced that fear of exposure will ensure Barnett will live up to his word. Back at McKenzie-Brackman, Leland in no uncertain terms lets Arthur Simon know that he will not be involved with political games and kicks the man out of his office.

(NOTE: Gary Sandy (Congressman Andrew Barnett) portrayed the program director of radio station WKRP in the situation comedy of the same name.)

Episode Fifty-Six

"Leave it to Geezer"

Written by Steven Bochco, David E. Kelley and Michele Gallery

Directed by Philip Goldfarb

Guest Stars: Lew Ayres (Henderson), Harry Caesar (Pike), Lou Jacobi (Sam), Charles Lane (Walter), Peter Turgeon (Harold), Dana Sparks (Jennifer Kepler), Nancy Vawter (Dorothy), Stan Kamber (Judge Shubow), Rod McCary (DiGrassi), Joe George (Judge Mueller), John Walter Davis (Pocklington), Jerry Hardin (D.A. Gold), Lizzie Maxwell (Bailiff), L. Scott Caldwell (Wanda), Roz Witt (Foreperson #2), T.J. Evans (Jimmy), Frank Renzulli (Dr. Romanelli), Gwynth Walsh (Melanie Hayes), Jan Devereaux (Burdick), Stephen Held (Cop #1), Denise Latella (Cop #2), Brian Libby (Peter Gaston), Paul Flick (Foreperson #1), Kevin Duffis (Clerk), Joanna Frank (Sheila Brackman), Coleby Lombardo (Alexander Brackman)

As if McKenzie isn't uptight enough about his relationship with Jennifer, right after a love making session he is gripped with pain that feels like a heart attack. He's rushed to the hospital where he learns that he just went through a bout of gas, which is very embarrassing. The strain is getting to be too much for him and McKenzie breaks off the relationship with Jennifer.

Due to the fact that Kuzak has been having so many problems with the court system, Sifuentes is given a case that normally would have gone to Michael. Kuzak, instead, is told to sit in on a contract dispute Becker is handling between film producer Melanie Hayes and her studio. Seeing this as the perfect opportunity to garner some publicity for himself, Becker wants to fight the battle in the press. Kuzak, on the other hand, offers a "softer" approach, which is infinitely more appealing to Melanie. The two sides, he notes, should work out a compromise. Apparently this is good advice, as everything works out perfectly and we are left with the impression that something *could* develop between Kuzak and Melanie.

As Van Owen is so often in a situation where her cases are deadly serious, it's a pleasure to see a change of pace story for her in this episode. It's her duty to prosecute four elderly men who robbed a bank that wouldn't give them their money because the nursing home they live in controls the purse strings. Their attorney, also extremely old and rather befuddled by everything that's going on, tries defending them, but it's difficult for him to keep his concentration on the matter at hand.

Van Owen is charmed by all of them, hardly looking on the defendants as violent criminals. Video footage clearly identifying the culprits is played for the jury, with Sam, Walter, Harold and Pike enjoying their images on the television screen. Van Owen offers a plea bargain, but lawyer Lorimar Henderson refuses to accept any concessions. He'll clear these men on his own, hopefully. The jury finds all four guilty and they fear going to jail. This was all done to add a little excitement to their lives, not to put them behind bars. Van Owen recommends suspended sentences, which is accepted by the judge. Before she leaves, she compliments Henderson on his summation, and the man is genuinely touched by her kindness.

Rollins gets some pointers from Kuzak in handling his first murder case. His client is Wanda Havens, charged with murdering her abusive husband. Rollins quickly establishes that Wanda and her children literally feared for their lives. Jimmy Havens is put on the stand, testifying that his father used to beat both him and his mother. Still, there seems to be some hesitation as the usually confident Jonathan begins to have his doubts. He is about to accept a plea bargain offered by the state, when he remembers that Kuzak said juries about to deliver a guilty verdict will not look at the accused. If the verdict is not guilty, you can sense it from the way they look at that person. This jury has all 12 sets of eyes locked directly on Wanda Havens. Rollins backs out of the plea bargain with Wanda's permission, and she is found not guilty, having acted in self defense. Once again Rollins has demonstrated just how good a lawyer he is and will continue to be.

Episode Fifty-Seven

"The Unbearable Lightness of Boring"

Written by David E. Kelley, William M. Finkelstein and Michele Gallery

Directed by Sandy Smolan

Guest Stars: Gwynyth Walsh (Melanie Hayes), Dana Andersen (Tammy), Renee Jones (Diana Moses), Gerald Anthony (Ross Burnett), Lucy Webb (Yolanda), Nancy Vawter (Dorothy Wyler), Dann Florek (Dave Meyer),

Camille Ameen (Natalie), Adam Silbar (Joshua Hennessey), Sue Rihr (Vicki), Jim Hudson (Seymour), Susan Silo (Yvette), Lenny Hicks (Daryl Tyler), Bob Corso (Al), Jim Jansen (Jerry), Charlie Callas (Sammy Frank), Kiel Martin (Frank Weiland), Peter Kevoian (D.A. Aoli), Apollo Dukakis (Judge Sardo), Kenneth Robert Shippy (Griffith)

As is the norm, Brackman's business practices are attacked by the partners and associates and he's had enough. As of that moment, Brackman will no longer handle the firm's day-to-day business as office manager. The job falls to Stuart Markowitz, who is convinced that he can do a more efficient job. Naturally it's only a short matter of time before Stuart's perfectionist style gets on the nerves of everyone, including Kelsey. They go to Brackman and beg him to take over as office manager again. Brackman, who's enjoying every moment of this, says that if he comes back, they're going to have to understand his position a little bit better. Everyone says that they will, and he steps back in, much to Stuart's chagrin.

Dave Meyer and Roxanne attend a ceremony where he receives the Direct Mail Man of the Year award. When he gets to the podium, as is his wont, Dave doesn't shut up, rambling on and on, including personal things about he and Roxanne. It concludes with his calling her up to the stage to stand beside her. Roxanne, feeling totally humiliated, leaves the ceremony, goes to Arnie and tells him that she wants a divorce.

Abby is offered $5,000 by Frank Weiland to get Mark Ross out of jail on a cocaine possession charge, with an additional $2,000 to come if she gets him out on bail. Since Van Owen is the one prosecuting Ross, Abby pleads with her to allow bail. Although she thinks it's a bad idea, out of friendship she works it out. Weiland is very impressed and tells Abby that he'll have a lot more work for her. Abby eventually gets the charges dropped for another of Weiland's friends, and Van Owen bursts her bubble by stating that Ross jumped bail and fled the country. At that moment, Abby begins to consider the fact that she's letting incoming cash cloud her judgement as an attorney. At the same time, she can't afford to stop.

Rollins is given the task of interviewing applicants for an internship position that's opened up, and he meets with the lovely, intelligent and enthusiastic Diana Moses. Rollins signs her up and finds himself very attracted to her. He is disappointed to learn that she's married.

A bombshell is dropped on Markowitz and Kelsey: the natural mother of their child, Tammy, wants her baby back. Ross Burnett explains that until the adoption is finalized, this is always a possibility. A meeting is arranged and it's clear that Tammy has no intention of backing down. She feels as though she's made a terrible mistake and wants to rectify it. Markowitz and Kelsey are ready to fight tooth and nail, and they enlist the aid of Becker and Sifuentes. Stuart wants them to do anything they can to discredit Tammy, which is extremely out of character for him, but an interesting touch nonetheless. To this end, they utilize private investigator Stephanie Hall. At episode's end, the couple is trying to prepare for the worst.

Episode Fifty-Eight

"His Suit is Hirsute"

Written by Steven Bochco, David E. Kelley, William M. Finkelstein and Michele Gallery

Directed by Win Phelps

Guest Stars: Gwynyth Walsh (Melanie Hayes), Michael Fairman (Judge McGrath), Joe Malone (Pastorini), Renee Jones (Diana Moses), Dana Andersen (Tammy Harris), Marco Rodriguez (Louis Vera), Douglas Roberts (Yzerman), Nancy Vawter (Dorothy Wyler), Alan Fudge (U.S. Attorney Flaherty), Mario Rocuzzo (Hilbar), Ross McKerras (Bradley), Ron Recasner (Jury Foreman), Barbara Tarbuck (Dr. Nagel), Rob Narita (Court Officer), Alan Britt (Officer #1), Rudy Prieto (Officer #2), Andrew Davis (Agent Lawrence), Bert L. Rogal (Judge Crea), Emily Kuroda (Ronnie), Helen Nemir Hanson (Agent Snow), Semina De Laurentis (Judge Davis), Gerald Anthony (Ross Burnett), Kiel Martin (Frank Weiland), Anthony Pena (Sergeant)

In the Markowitz/Kelsey case, Sifuentes puts Tammy Harris on the stand and does everything he can to make her seem like an unfit mother. What he doesn't expect is that her attorney, Richard Yzerman, has done his homework as well. When he puts Kelsey on the witness stand, he brings up such damaging issues as her long working hours, the desperate search for a nanny and the rocky relationship between her and her own mother. Sifuentes brings in Dr. Nagel, who testifies that the removal of the child at this time could be emotionally scarring for life. Yzerman jumps on this as well, letting the judge know that Nagel is receiving $3,000 for participating in the proceedings.

Feeling that things are too close to call, Sifuentes tells Markowitz he's going to make the closing argument, because the judge would feel more sympathetic toward him. Stuart pours his heart out to him about the love he and his wife share, and the bond they've developed with the baby. The judge finds in favor of Tammy Harris. The child is immediately returned to her. Nobody ever said that *L.A. Law* was a show that guaranteed a happy ending.

Diana Moses tells Rollins that she and

her husband are breaking up. While on the inside he may be jumping up and down, Rollins acts as the sensitive friend and offers any assistance he can provide.

Abby is discussing an upcoming trial with Weiland, when narcotic officers break in and arrest him. Abby is able to persuade the judge to let the man out on jail, despite the Deputy D.A.'s opposition. It's Abby's opinion that Weiland should work out a plea bargain, because the D.A.'s office has a witness to his drug transactions. Weiland tells her not to worry about it and, indeed, when this witness (Louis Perez) gets up to testify, he says he made up the entire story.

It's not until later that we and Abby learn that Weiland threatened the lives of Perez's children. Weiland is off the hook and in gratitude for all she's done, he pays Abby her $10,000 fee and tries to give her a bonus $10,000. She rejects the latter, because he's a man who could possibly kill someone else's children and she can't in any conscience defend a person like that. The police break in with a warrant to arrest Abby. The money she was paid is drug money, and it's a crime to launder illegally gotten cash.

While things are heating up between Kuzak and Melanie Hayes, as well as cooling off between he and Van Owen, Kuzak is in the midst of a trial. He represents Walter Hilbar, who charges a man named Bradley with installing a heating system that exploded, nearly taking his life. Frank Pastorini, Bradley's lawyer, provides a wide range of humorous approaches to the trial to take the jury's collective mind off the seriousness of the situation. Kuzak feels as though he's going to lose another case and he's determined it will not happen. In response to Pastorini's escapades, Kuzak delivers his summation dressed in the gorilla suit he crashed Grace's wedding in during sea-son one. Before concluding, Kuzak removes the mask and makes the point that although certain aspects of the trial may have been perceived as humorous and entertaining, Walter Hilbar was nearly killed due to Bradley's negligence. The effect is perfect and the jury finding for Hilbar with a very large settlement.

Episode Fifty-Nine

"America the Beautiful"

Written by David E. Kelley, William M. Finkelstein, Michele Gallery and Judith Parker

Directed by Max Tash

Guest Stars: Dann Florek (Dave Meyer), Renee Jones (Diana Moses), Wayne Tippit (Leo Hackett), Nancy Vawter (Dorothy Wyler), Stanley Grover (Judge Richard Lobel), Alan Fudge (U.S. Attorney Flaherty), Olivia Cole (Judge MacFarland), Patricia Gaul (Lorraine Mack), Buck Flower (Henry Broder), Terry Bozeman (Jeffries), Don Sparks (Russell Spitzer), Fausto Bara (Father Higuera), Richard Assad (Grand Jury Foreperson), Gordon Ross (Jury Foreperson), Robert V. Barron (Leonard), Henry Harris (Edward), Clare Nono (Christine Acker), Tinaki (Homeless Woman #1), Chip Heller (Manager), Stan Yale (Homeless Man), Bruce Fairbairn (Bernie Lustig), Amanda Plummer (Alice Hackett), Sharon Conley (Homeless Woman #2), Cal Gibson (Reporter)

Kuzak represents Abby in her case against the narcs who arrested her. U.S. Attorney Flaherty has no qualms about attacking her in court and it comes to the point where Abby is willing to appear in front of a Grand Jury, although Kuzak isn't crazy about the idea. Flaherty does everything he can to discredit Abby. She is given the opportunity to speak for herself and drives home the point that the prosecuting counsel was unable to prove that any of her clients were drug dealers. If this is the case, how can he determine the money she received was laundered drug money? The point is made and the charges dropped. McKenzie is particularly impressed with this turn of events, apologizes for thinking that Abby wouldn't be right for partner material and asks her to come back to the firm. Although she plays hard to get, Abby ultimately agrees and happily so.

Kelsey cannot overcome the pain she's feeling over having lost her nearly-adopted daughter, while Markowitz feels they have to push on. Meanwhile, Diana Moses' divorce is not going as smoothly as she had hoped, so she asks Jonathan Rollins if he can lend a helping hand.

New client Leo Hackett is so impressed with the way that Benny is able to function among his co-workers and lead a fairly normal life, that he asks him to meet his daughter, Alice. She, too, is retarded, but very shy and withdrawn. Benny gets together with her and the two of them hit it off, particularly after she teaches him how to drive.

Roxanne and Becker proceed with her divorce from Dave Meyer, who tries his best to get Arnie disqualified due to a conflict of interest. The judge rules that if an out-of-court settlement is reached, Arnie can represent Roxanne. However, if it goes to trial, then she will need another lawyer. Roxanne doesn't want to drag this thing through the courts, but Becker emphasizes that there are millions of dollars worth of royalties from Meyer's video business that she deserves a portion of.

Van Owen is in the midst of trying to prosecute Richard Jeffries in the murder of a transient named Vincent Kyle. Little help can be gained from friends of Kyle or a local priest, Father Sul-

livan, who is almost fanatical in his cause for the homeless. Another homeless man, Henry Broder, who was with Kyle the night of his death, testifies that they were rummaging through Jeffries' trash cans for food when Jeffries came outside and started shooting at Vincent.

Richard Spitzer, representing Jeffries, points out that Kyle had a history of mental illness, erratic behavior and attempted suicides. During all of this, Father Sullivan continually screams out in the court. Privately, Van Owen tells him he's hurting their case more than helping it.

Jeffries takes the stand, saying Kyle came at him with a knife. Fearing for the lives of himself and his family, Jeffries did what he had to do to protect them. Neighbors of Jeffries testify that the homeless take drugs, urinate in public and fight with each other. The jury, perhaps fearful of "these people" as well, find that Jeffries acted properly given the threatening situation. Father Sullivan leads the attending homeless people through choruses of "America, The Beautiful."

Episode Sixty

"Urine Trouble Now"

Written by David E. Kelley, William M. Finkelstein, Michele Gallery and Judith Parker

Directed by Rob Thompson

Guest Stars: Amanda Plummer (Alice Hackett), Wayne Tippit (Leo Hackett), Nancy Vawter (Dorothy Wyler), Dann Florek (Dave Meyer), Lenny Hicks (Daryl Tyler), Renee Jones (Diana Moses), Vonna Bowen (Stenographer), Steven Flynn (Ellis Agnew), Bruce Fairbairn (Sheldon Ganz), Bruce A. Young (Edward Rice), Carlos Romero (Alfredo Perez), Robert King (Gatling), Richard Holden (Geoffrey Norman), Anne Haney (Judge Travelini), Joaquin

Martinez (Montoya), Tony Plana (Rivera), George Coe (Judge Wallace R. Vance), "Rocky" Turner Wilson, Jr. (Melvin Redding), Sean Thomas (Eddie Williams)

During deposition, Dave Meyer sics his lawyer, Sheldon Ganz, on Roxanne. The first thing that Ganz does is describe her financial situation in life prior to marriage. At roughly the same time, Dave accuses Arnie Becker of being a traitor. Off the record, Becker states that despite the business relationship that exists between the two men, Roxanne is his primary concern and he will do whatever he has to in order to make sure she's treated fairly.

Dave is forced to admit that he is not completely comfortable with the idea of letting Roxanne out of his life, but she explains—as gently as possible—that their marriage was a mistake and no amount of money in the world will change the fact that it's over. Having no choice but to accept this, Meyer signs the divorce papers and Roxanne is given $825,000. He tells her he'll always love her. Markowitz lays out a financial plan that will allow her never to work again, but Rox feels that she can't leave McKenzie-Brackman. It's the one thing in her life that has purpose.

As Rollins helps Diana Moses through her divorce, a romantic relationship starts to develop. Brackman is the partner who first gets wind of this and he suggests to Rollins that getting involved with a co-worker might be a mistake. Although put off by this statement, Rollins takes the time to point out the fact that Markowitz and Kelsey are married, while Leland McKenzie had a relationship with a client's *granddaughter*. Following this, he tells Brackman to mind his own business.

Sifuentes represents Oscar Montoya, owner of a Mexican brewery who turned down a purchase offer by Gatling Distributors. Since that time, Gatling has deliberately spread rumors that Mexican workers urinate in the beer before it is distributed to stores and taverns. As unlikely a scenario as this is, the story has nonetheless caused sales to plummet. Sifuentes presents witnesses who actually heard Gatling tell his employees to spread the malicious rumor. Beyond the business issue at stake, says Sifuentes to the jury, they must consider the racial connotations of such a story. The case is ultimately settled.

The Sensations and their leader, Melvin Redding, have gone to Kuzak to help protect their name. Some years earlier the band sold the rights to its name and material to a group called The New Sensations. What they didn't expect was that this new incarnation would, in their opinion, change their work in the attempt to modernize it. Melvin wants to take the band on a national tour, but Eddie Wiltern, leader of The New Sensations, hates the idea and is suing for breach of contract. The only way that both sides feel they can make Judge Vance see their point is if they perform samples of their music.

The Original Sensations do a calm, smooth, nostalgic number, while The New Sensations perform a loud and somewhat lyrically vulgar song, accompanied by gyrating hips and suggestive dance movements. Upon viewing both sets of performers, Judge Vance comes to his decision quickly. Each can keep the name, because there is absolutely no way that the public would ever mix the two of them up.

Episode Sixty-One

"Consumed Innocent"

Written by David E. Kelley, William M. Finkelstein, Michele Gallery, Judith Parker

Directed by Win Phelps

Guest Stars: Amanda Plummer (Alice

Hackett), Wayne Tippit (Leo Hackett), Renee Jones (Diana Moses), Nancy Vawter (Dorothy Wyler), Joyce Hyser (Allison Gottlieb), Bruce Fairbairn (Sheldon Ganz), J.T. Walsh (Pete Bostik), Daniel Ziskie (McCleish), Earl Boen (Judge Swanson), Keith Mills (Judge Green), Wendy Cutler (Moira Noonan), Don Keith Opper (Kevin Garwood), Laura Leigh Hughes (Zoe Lazar), Paul Napier (Leonard Kaiser), Armin Shimerman (Timothy Wiseboro)

Allison asks Sifuentes to help her out of a situation in which she was making a commercial and the "Star's" python ate one of his co-stars, a pig. Each animal owner believes the other guilty of negligence. Trying to deal as best he can with a horrible case of the flu, Sifuentes meets with the animal owners. During this meeting, Wiseboro (the snake owner) is called and told his python has died. Shocked, he announces that he's going to sue Allison as well as pig owner Zifrin, claiming the pig was a kind of poison that killed his pet. The man plans for a "decent" funeral, but Sifuentes demands an autopsy. Wiseboro, feeling that it wouldn't be right not to bury his beloved pet right away, agrees to work out a settlement, while Sifuentes agrees to go home and "die" from his flu.

When Leo Hackett sees Benny kissing his daughter, Alice, he grows furious, feeling he's taking advantage of her. Leo goes to see Brackman about this, telling him to inform Benny that he shouldn't go near Alice anymore. Brackman does indeed talk to Benny, but in a fatherly way, telling Benny to take things slowly and not force Alice to do anything she doesn't want to do. Benny gives his word. When Leo sees that things haven't changed, he threatens to pull all of his business away from McKenzie-Brackman. Leo finally talks to Alice about *her* feelings and he comes to realize that she really does care about Benny. Leo apologizes to

Brackman for the tactics he tried to use earlier.

Van Owen is prosecuting television talk show host Pete Bostik—a Robert Downey, Jr.-type character—who is charged with inciting his show's audience to kill activist Leonard Kaiser. Bostik, who seems to think that he's somewhat invincible due to the popularity of his show, feels the trial will just give the series more publicity. In court throughout the entire trial are a variety of his fans who chant his name at every opportunity they can.

Van Owen puts audience member Zoe Lazar on the stand and she describes the way that Pete fired up the audience against his guest. Next, the jury sees a clip from that particular show with Pete suggesting the audience take their fight with Kaiser to the parking lot, which, tragically, they did. One of those found guilty of manslaughter is Kevin Garwood, who is called to the stand and boasts that his hero gave him the opportunity to be as violent as he wanted to be in front of the camera. Garwood doesn't realize just how much damage he's doing to Pete.

On the stand himself, Pete Bostik boasts that the American public will never stand for his incarceration. Van Owen responds that they'll forget him quickly enough and move on to the next big thing, while he rots in jail. The jury finds him guilty as charged, and he begs Van Owen to help him get a light sentence; that his television persona is just an act. The "honest" expression of feeling comes too late. Van Owen honestly believes that the Pete Bostiks of the world are a dangerous threat and she is going to recommend the maximum penalty.

At the McKenzie-Brackman Christmas party, Kuzak and Van Owen try to iron things out between them while Ann Kelsey gets a phone call from her doctor, who informs her that she's pregnant. She and Stuart Markowitz are overjoyed, and *L.A. Law*'s third season ends on an uplifting note.

SEASON FOUR

PRODUCTION STAFF
Executive Producer: David E. Kelley
Co-Executive Producer: Rick Wallace
Supervising Producer: William M. Finkelstein
Producer: Michael M. Robin
Producer: Elodie Keene
Coordinating Producer: Alice West

REGULAR CAST
Harry Hamlin: Michael Kuzak
Susan Dey: Grace Van Owen
Jill Eikenberry: Ann Kelsey
Alan Rachins: Douglas Brackman, Jr.
Michele Greene: Abby Perkins
Jimmy Smits: Victor Sifuentes
Michael Tucker: Stuart Markowitz
Susan Ruttan: Roxanne Melman
Richard Dysart: Leland McKenzie
Blair Underwood: Jonathan Rollins
Larry Drake: Benny Stulwicz
Diana Muldaur: Rosalind Shays

Episode Sixty-Two

"The Unsterile Cuckoo"

Written by David E. Kelley

Directed by Rob Thompson

Guest Stars: Amanda Plummer (Alice Hackett), Wayne Tippit (Leo Hackett), Bruce Ornstein (John Trischuta), John Hancock (Judge Richard Armand), George Murdock (Samuel Wikpod), Sheila Shaw (Animal Activist #1), Keith McDaniel (Animal Activist #2), Joyce Hyser (Allison Gottlieb), Mitch Carter (Richard Calder), Thomas Nelson Webb (Tom Islander), Noreen Hennessy (Maureen Lacker), Terri Semper (Marcia), Julie Payne (Ellen Barrett), John Lehne (Kenneth Randall), Steven Barr (Steve), Robert Crow (Bob), Margaret Nagle (Mary), John Lantz (Derrick), Patrick Waddell (Foreperson), Bill Hollis (Animal Activist #3), Bruce Marchiano (Catcher), Brad Peterson (Umpire), Mary Ingersoll (Animal Activist #4), Bruce Taylor (Animal Activist #5), Kim Murdock (Reporter #1), Kevin Roberts (Reporter #2), Wayne Hackett (3rd Baseman)

Leo Hackett is extremely distraught when he learns that Benny and Alice have been sleeping together. To make sure she doesn't get pregnant, as he suspects that she would not be able to handle motherhood, he makes an appointment for her to be sterilized. Arnie Becker and Abby Perkins go to McKenzie hoping he'll speak to Leo about how wrong this is. Both McKenzie and Brackman are against the idea of interfering in Leo's personal life, although McKenzie eventually speaks to the man about the situation. Leo hears his words and says he'll drop the idea of sterilization, *if* McKenzie can make sure that Benny will use contraception during sex.

A softball game with a $5,000 payoff fills the minds of most of the employees of McKenzie-Brackman. The only person having trouble in terms of playing is Markowitz, because a big game falls on the same night as one of his Lamaze classes. Kelsey says he should present his "case" before the other couples to get their opinion, and that he should abide by what they say. Confident they'll see things his way, he agrees. During the next Lamaze class he explains what's going on to everyone and they give him his blessing. During the game, however, he comes back to the Lamaze class, feeling that being a father is a hell of a lot more important than playing a softball game.

Despite his opposition to the idea, Sifuentes is saddled with the case of furrier Kenneth Randall, who has been suffering the wrath of the Save the Animals Foundation. That organization's attorney, John Trischuta, wants to show the jury a video tape of animals being brutally killed in steel traps so their pelts can be taken and made into coats. Sifuentes objects, but is overruled and the tape is shown. Putting organization head Ellen Barrett on the stand, Sifuentes gets her to admit that it is certainly illegal to splash animal blood on people who decide they want to wear fur coats. Sifuentes should know from whence he speaks, because he becomes a victim of a similar incident and is totally shocked by it.

What he emphasizes is the fact that while members of the Save the Animals Foundation have a right to protest, Kenneth Randall has an equal right to produce and sell furs. The jury comes back in favor of the organization. Judge Armand feels that, given the evidence, the jury had no reason to do so. Sifuentes is told that his client can be given a new trial. Randall has had enough, however, and wants to cut a deal with Save the Animals. Sifuentes, who didn't want the case in the first place, is frustrated because of the amount in legal fees that were lost by his not winning.

113

Episode Sixty-Three

"Captain Hurt"

Written by William M. Finkelstein

Directed by Win Phelps

Guest Stars: Veronica Cartwright (Margaret Flanagan), Jennifer Hetrick (Corrinne Hammond), Ashleigh Sterling (Chloe Hammond), Lorinne Vozoff (Chloe Hammond), John Morrissey (Judge Roberta Harbin), Carl Lumbly (Earl Williams), Vonetta McGee (Jackie Williams), Randy Oglesby (Leonard Knipp), Marnie McPhail (Amy Slesin), Cedering Foz (TV Anchor), Tricia O'Neil (Meredith Korngold), Reid Cruickshanks (Al Metoyer), George Buck (Les Corry), Oceana Marr (Enid Simpson), Bruce Newbold (Reporter on TV), Gary Blumsack (Stuart Zaplin), Natalie Core (Helen), Michael Bofshever (Phil), Rudy Challenger (Claude Nevins), John Hostetter (William Forrester), Arva Holt (Judge Cynthia Kraman), Kate Randolph Burns (Clerk—Kuzak's Case), Martin West (Sgt. Hill), Sally Champlin (Foreperson), Dana Gladstone (Dr. Fuller), Tim De Zarn (Voltaggio), Lisa Wolpe (Irma Vytek), Dayna Winston (Janine Williams), Stewart Wilson-Turner (Earl Williams, Jr.), Janice Ryan (Reporter), Ilona Wilson (Lorna Bruck)

Becker discovers that the husband of client Corrinne Hammond is the owner of a very successful architectural firm. Corrinne wants to work out a quick and amicable divorce, but Brackman emphasizes the firm's sluggish earnings and wants Arnie to go for the proverbial jugular. Just so her husband understands how serious Corrinne is, Becker has the locks on her home changed and then has the police arrest him for breaking and entering. This upsets Corrinne, who once again tells him she doesn't want this divorce to be an ugly one.

Becker finds out Randy Hammond had been given a "general" discharge from the Army, but Corrinne won't give him any more details. He has Roxanne do some research and during a subsequent meeting says that Corrinne wants a $750,000 settlement. Randy balks at the idea, until Becker mentions something about the fact he had been discharged from the Army because of a homosexual affair he was involved. in.

Randy immediately assumes Corrinne told him about this, and Corrinne's reaction—after picking up the check—is to be furious with Becker for making this divorce something she didn't want it to be, particularly because the couple's daughter, Chloe, now has to live in a hostile environment.

Sifuentes takes Benny out to buy his first set of condoms and has no embarrassment over the idea, until the woman clerk at the store assumes they are gay lovers.

Van Owen is prosecuting Leonard Kniff for falsifying insurance claims. His attorney claims Kniff is suffering from a masochistic disorder that forces him to obey his secretary's every command, whether the orders concern sex or criminal activity. He simply cannot help himself. Van Owen puts Knipp on the witness stand and really laces in to him. It's obvious the man is being turned on by the way she's snapping at him. Turning to the jury, she asks that they see through the charade Kniff is going through to protect his criminal actions. During this little speech, Kniff shouts out that he wants Van Owen to hurt him. The jury finds Knipp guilty, and the man doesn't ask for bail. He wants to be locked up. In fact, he wants to be Van Owen's slave.

Black college professor Earl Williams is defended by Kuzak. Williams, who Kuzak truly does believe in, is charged with murdering his white assistant, Nina Corry. Damaging his defense is the fact that a supposed eyewitness steps forward and identifies Williams.

Then Nina's father steps forward and attests that Williams had been sleeping with his daughter. Prosecuting attorney Margaret Flanagan investigates further and finds that the semen found in Nina's body is indeed Williams'. In private, Kuzak, who had no idea he was sleeping with the victim, demands that Earl tell him everything that went on between them. Reluctantly, Williams admits that he made love to Nina the day of her murder, but insists he did not commit the crime.

(This begins what is easily L.A. Law's *longest trial, spreading out over numerous episodes. In a sense, all of Michael Kuzak's convictions that we have seen over the past three seasons come to a head here. Never has he been more passionate about someone than he is in this story line. Veronica Cartwright (Margaret Flanagan) has starred in a wide variety of motion pictures, includi*Alien *and* The Witches of Eastwick. *Carl Lumbly (Earl Williams) is best known to television fans as Petrie on* Cagney and Lacey.)

Episode Sixty-Four

"When Irish Eyes Are Smiling"

Written by David E. Kelley and William M. Finkelstein

Directed by David Carson

Guest Stars: Dion Anderson (Lester Craig), Dayna Winston (Janine Williams), Stewart Wilson-turner (Earl Williams Jr.), Lorinne Vozoff (Judge Roberta Harbin), Carl Lumbly (Earl Williams), Vonetta McGee (Jackie Williams), Jennifer Hetrick (Corrinne Hammond), Veronica Cartwright (Margaret Flanagan), Ashleigh Sterling (Chloe Hammond), Richard Riehle (Edmund Clancy), Jan Munroe (Detective Roman Vitale), Reid Cruickshanks (Foreperson), Jon Matthews (Mr. Kopesky), Kate Randolph Burns (Clerk), David Michael Sterling (Court Officer), Mary Jackson (Mildred Weedon)

Due to the fact the entire settlement would be approximately $10,000, Rollins has no choice but to turn down the case of Mildred Weedon, who was denied insurance for something she should have been covered for. Sensing the woman's desperation, as she has been unable to secure the services of a law firm of any merit, he agrees to make a phone call for her. Rollins contacts insurance adjustor Edmund Clancy, who is full of himself and convinced the case is so small that McKenzie-Brackman won't touch it.

When Brackman finds out about Jonathan even looking at this case, he gives him a hard time until Rollins details Clancy's general attitude. Assuming the whole thing won't take more than an hour or so, Brackman offers to step in to negotiate a better deal. Clancy comes up with an extra $1,000. Rollins gets wind of this, comes into the conference room and starts screaming at Clancy, threatening "I'll see you in court!" When he leaves, Clancy turns to Brackman and tries laughing it off, assuming that Jonathan will be reprimanded.

Brackman kind of shrugs it off, explaining that sometimes Jonathan Rollins can't be controlled. But he's a lawyer that hardly ever loses, so they can't afford to fire him either. Moments later, Brackman enters Jonathan's office with a check from Clancy for $12,000. The little "scene" worked exactly as planned.

Diana Moses is a student in Leland McKenzie's law class and by the way he goes at the students, and her in particular, she feels he is trying to drive her away from the firm because of her relationship with Rollins. At the office, McKenzie is as polite and nurturing as he always is, which confuses her. During a conversation, he admits that he's

115

hard in the classroom because he's trying to help create lawyers. But in the office, he wants to build confidence and loyalty among his people. While he doesn't necessarily approve of her relationship with Rollins, he would nonetheless hate to lose her.

In an effort to apologize to Corrinne Hammond for getting so rough in her divorce settlement with husband Randy, Becker offers to take her out to lunch. They go out several more times and it's obvious they're starting to connect romantically. McKenzie voices his concern about how unethical it is for Becker to be involved with one of his clients. Arnie agrees, relates this to Corrinne and suggests that she find a new attorney.

While trying to deal with the fact that her husband has been unfaithful, Jackie Williams nonetheless takes the stand and claims that Earl was with her at the time of Nina Corry's death. Kuzak puts Detective Vitale on the stand and the officer states that in his opinion. Williams did not kill Nina. Opposing counsel Margaret Flanagan does whatever she can to discredit Vitale's testimony, noting he is bitter about the police force because he was passed up for a promotion. Flanagan then offers to reduce Williams' charges to second degree murder, but the man refuses to accept this "compromise." Williams himself is put on the stand, and Flanagan questions him in regard to killing Nina Corry when she wanted to break off their relationship. Kuzak objects, but Flanagan nonetheless continues trying to provoke a violent reaction from him. While the Williams family tries to cope with the issue of Earl's being unfaithful to Jackie, the jury comes back with a guilty verdict.

Episode Sixty-Five

"The Mouse That Soared"

Written by David E. Kelley and Wil-

liam Finkelstein

Directed by Sandy Smolan

Guest Stars: David Rappaport (Hamilton Schuyler), Veronica Cartwright (Margaret Flanagan), Carl Lumbly (Earl Williams), Vonetta McGee (Jackie Williams), Lorinne Vozoff (Judge Roberta Harbin), Jim Haynie (Judge Nelson Dunley), Jane Daly (Connie), Tom O'Rourke (Harold Stevens), Tommy Madden (Adam Creland), Eric Sever (Garry Lowell), Lana Koss (Kevin Riley), Charles Martiniz (Patron), Jennifer Karr (Cynthia Halp), Ellen Blake (Elizabeth Brand), Daniel Hutchison (Phillip Holden), Richardson Morse (Dr. Platt), Charlie Holliday (Foreperson)

Due to a shortage of available lawyers, Markowitz is given a simple litigation trial to handle. To help him get up to speed, Arnie loans out Roxanne, who is dreading the assignment. Stuart Markowitz is a great guy, but he is such a perfectionist who worries about every little detail, that he drives everybody crazy. Roxanne's fears prove correct as Markowitz has her deal with reams and reams of paper, color coding of the files and so on. Finally, Abby offers a little constructive advice. He should be prepared, definitely, but being overprepared will only show the jury and the court that he is inexperienced. Stuart thanks her for the assistance.

A good friend of Kelsey, named Connie, asks her to take on her daughter's case. The girl was harassed by a right-to-life organization after she had an abortion. Out of friendship, Kelsey agrees to take on the case, but there is concern at McKenzie-Brackman. Research shows that numerous clients would leave the firm if Kelsey was to take a side in the pro-choice/right-to-life argument. She has no choice but to drop it, although she considers the idea of starting their own practice with Markowitz. He doesn't agree. He'd prefer

Larry Drake portrays Benny Stulwicz, the developmentally-handicapped mail clerk who nonetheless frequently teaches the high-powered lawyers a few lessons.

Husband-and-wife lawyers Ann Kelsey and Stuart Markowitz (at left portrayed by Michael Tucker and Jill Eikenberry) get free direct-mail marketing advice from whiz Dave Meyer (Portrayed by Dann Florek). Secretary Roxanne Melman (Susan Ruttan) looks on.

to stay just where they are.

Sifuentes comes up against Hamilton Schuyler, the midget lawyer he butted heads with the previous season. Sifuentes has been asked by restaurant owner Harold Stevens to stop dwarf-throwing contests at a nearby establishment. When Sifuentes learns that opposing counsel will be Schuyler, he immediately becomes concerned about the man's habit of using his size as an advantage in manipulating the jury. Judge Nelson Dunley warns both of them to conduct themselves in the best of decorum in his courtroom.

Both lawyers agree, wagering a dinner on who will win. In a sense, for Sifuentes it's a no-win scenario. He tries to show that dwarf-throwing should be banned, but Schuyler's arguments are impossible to beat. First off, one of the dwarfs takes the stand and states that there aren't many employment opportunities available for him, and by partaking in dwarf throwing he can bring in as much as $500 a night.

Then Schuyler notes that wet tee shirt contests aren't deemed by society to be degrading to women, so dwarf-throwing shouldn't be to dwarfs. In terms of safety, more people are injured in football games each year than in dwarf-throwing. Schuyler wins the case and enjoys a scrumptious dinner supplied by Sifuentes.

(NOTE: David Rappaport makes his second appearance as Hamilton Schuyler in this episode, and the chemistry between he and Jimmy Smits (Sifuentes) is just wonderful. One can imagine that we would have seen more of him in the course of the series. Tragically, Rappaport, suffering from severe depression, killed himself in 1990.)

Kuzak receives the testimony of convicted drug dealer Phil Holden, who claims he saw the man who murdered Nina Corry and that it was *not* Earl Williams. Holden passes a lie detector test and Kuzak goes before Judge Harbin in an attempt to get Williams a new trial. Margaret Flanagan doesn't agree, informing the judge of Holden's criminal activities and that Kuzak, in exchange for the man's testimony, will represent him on his drug charges. The judge considers all of this and rules that Holden's testimony cannot be seen as credible, therefore there are no grounds for a new trial. Kuzak explodes over this and is arrested for his trouble so that he can have the opportunity to calm down.

Episode Sixty-Six

"One Rat-One Ranger"

Fifty pounds of canteloupe arrive in the office thanks to Brackman. It's his hope that the partners and associates will eat healthier. What he doesn't expect is a large rat to come out of the crate and escape. A comedy of errors ensues as people try to capture it and an exterminator is called. Eventually the rat is caught in a rat trap, and Benny is upset that the little critter is dead. Abby tries to console him by saying the rat is in heaven. "My mom is in heaven," Benny cries out. She corrects herself, stating that it's actually rat heaven.

Markowitz's first litigation case goes to trial. He's representing a dating service being sued by Dianna Dorian, who claims the company didn't live up to its promise. Markowitz objects to every detail, which causes the judge to warn him to selectively object. Markowitz reconsiders his approach to the case and shocks everyone by becoming a master of the game. He essentially causes Dianna to admit that she's extremely lonely but has such high standards that it's impossible for anyone to meet them. He puts Dianna's former date Howard Hulse up on the stand, and Hulse, who seems like a nice enough guy, is torn apart by her.

The jury finds in the dating service's favor, and Dianna actually thanks Markowitz for making her reconsider certain aspects of herself. As they're leaving the courtroom, Markowitz bumps in to Dave Meyer, introduces him to Dianna and it seems that the two of them hit it off immediately.

The firm is in serious financial trouble and both McKenzie and Brackman feel they have to bring in a new partner to provide additional clients and boost revenues. They interview Rosalind Shays and, despite objections from Becker and Kelsey, she is ultimately made a partner.

Van Owen is prosecuting Ed Haley, accused of sexually molesting his five-year-old daughter, Lisa. Ed's ex-wife, Charlotte, has attested that after spending a weekend with her father, Lisa came home with bruises on the inside of her thighs. Ed's argument is that she slipped and fell on her bicycle, but the D.A.'s office feels otherwise. To support this claim, Van Owen calls in Dr. Bizland, who claims that the scar tissue on the little girl's legs more likely resulted from molestation than anything else. Ed's attorney, Brian La Porte, argues that the evidence isn't conclusive, therefore isn't valid.

Van Owen feels as though she has no choice but to call Lisa to the stand, and there the little girl uses a doll to show the jury where her father supposedly touched her. La Porte points out that Charlotte coached Lisa, so the jury really can't take her testimony seriously. Indeed, Ed Haley is found not guilty and he is given full visitation rights. In private, Charlotte tells Grace Van Owen that since the system let her down, she's got no choice but to take Lisa and disappear so that Ed can't lay his hands on her again.

For once, Van Owen has to agree with her client in terms of breaking the law.

The system broke down once again, and this seems to be the only logical solution.

Episode Sixty-Seven

"Lie Down and Deliver"

Written by Christopher Keyser and Amy Lippman

Directed by Gabrielle Beaumont

Guest Stars: Dann Florek (Dave Meyer), Connie Mercede (Denise DiNapoli), Felicity LaFortune (Leah Adair), Bruce Fairbairn (Sheldon Ganz), Joyce Hyser (Allison Gottlieb), Jennifer Hetrick (Corrinne Hammond), Stan Kamber (Judge Harlan Shubow), Richmond Hoxie (Edward Powell), Keith Mills (Judge Walter Green), Richard Cox (Curtis Haber), Joshua Bryant (Dr. Gregory Stark), Patrick DeSantis (Monty), Lisa Dinkins (Foreperson), George D. Wallace (Judge Peter Brosens), Susan Gibney (Lucy Blanchard), Leilani Sarelle (Cheryl Flecksor), Stephen Tobolowsky (Dr. Michael Segal)

Arnie Becker and Dave Meyer are sued over their do-it-yourself video. Denise DiNapoli argues that she followed the advice offered in the video to the letter, but ended up with a terrible settlement so now wants damages. Becker mentions what's going on at the staff meeting, and the partners warn him they will not be a part of the lawsuit. This infuriates Becker, because his partners were so willing to take a percentage of the profits but don't want anything to do with the suit.

Making things even more difficult is the fact that Becker and Meyer are constantly fighting, mostly due to Roxanne's divorce settlement. Finally they reconcile as Dave admits that he didn't get involved with Arnie for the money but rather for the friendship, and Becker admits that he has benefitted, not just financially, from knowing him. From this point of unification, they are able to negotiate a fair settlement with Denise DiNapoli.

Brackman wins $5,000 from a cereal contest, as do hundreds of others. The cereal company, admitting that there was a printing error, only wants to pay the winners $100 each. Brackman hates the idea and rounds up 100 winners who are children. Once this is done, company attorney Ed Powell realizes that the negative publicity of going to trial will be more damaging than paying each winner. They settle at $1,200 per person, including Brackman. Everyone is happy.

Kelsey defends Dr. Michael Segal, charged with negligence in the stillborn death of a woman's child. Kelsey uses her own pregnancy as a tool in the trial, but when she puts the mother on the stand, she attacks the woman for drinking and smoking during pregnancy, both of which she knew could conceivably be dangerous. Abby, who has witnessed all this, feels that Kelsey just came off as an attacker. Rather than gain sympathy from the jury, she alienated it.

Kuzak is told of what happened and he wants Abby to take the trial from that point on, much to Kelsey's anger. Opposing counsel calls Dr. Stark to the stand and in his estimation, Segal was negligent. Abby lets the jury know that Stark makes his living by being a professional witness in malpractice suits. Segal is offered a settlement that is substantially lower than the amount called for in the original suit. Segal stands by the fact that he did nothing wrong and he will not accept any charges that will damage his reputation. He'd rather see what the jury decides.

Ann Kelsey delivers the closing argument, apologizing if her passion had gotten the best of her earlier. She tells the jury she fears something happening to her unborn child as well, but that

fear, and the reality that some children are stillborn, does not mean that Dr. Segal was negligent in the performance of his duty. The jury agrees, as Segal is found not guilty. Abby and Kelsey work out their differences regarding the trial, and their friendship is back on track.

Rosalind Shays has dinner with Victor Sifuentes and Allison Gottlieb. Sifuentes is expecting the worst, but, instead, Rosalind flatters him and charms him into lowering all of his defenses. When Rosalind excuses herself to the ladies room, Sifuentes turns to Allison and compliments the woman. Allison laughs, unable to believe that Victor fell for the b.s. that Rosalind was handing out. Simply put, Allison doesn't trust her.

(NOTE: Diana Muldaur (Rosalind Shays) is a veteran actress who co-starred on Star Trek: The Next Generation *during its second season as Dr. Pulaski.)*

Episode Sixty-Eight

"Placenta Claus is Coming to Town"

Written by William M. Finkelstein and Cynthia Saunders

Directed by Rob Thompson

Guest Stars: Amanda Plummer (Alice Hackett), Veronica Cartwright (Margaret Flanagan), Lorainse Vozoff (Judge Roberta Harbin), Joyce Hyser (Allison Gottlieb), Carl Lumbly (Earl Williams), Vonetta McGee (Jackie Williams), Wayne Tippit (Leo Hackett), Jennifer Hetrick (Corrinne Hammond), Ashleigh Sterling (Chloe Hammond), Reid Cruickshanks (Al Metoyer), Stacy Edwards (Nicole Corry), Dayna Winston (Janine Williams), Stewart Wilson-Turner (Earl Williams, Jr.), Rebecca Stanley (D. Wallace), Philip Persons (Dr. Ernest Keller), Martha Velez (Gloria Stilton), George Buck (Less Corry), Lillian Lehman (Judge Mary

Harcourt), Gary Blumsack (Stuart Za-plin), Warren Stanhope (Dr. Parks), Martin Garner (Mordechai), Kate Randolph Burns (Clerk), Skip O'Brien (Driver), Beah Richards (Eleanor Williams), Bill Feeney (Guard), Richard Grove (Teamster), James Higgins (John Keyes)

Benny gets permission from Leo Hackett to marry Alice and Alice says yes to the proposal.

Corrinne Hammond informs Becker than her ex-husband insists on having Chloe for Christmas, even though the agreement says she is to be with her mother. Becker goes before Judge Harcourt and is reprimanded for sleeping with his client. She is told to get a new lawyer. Later, Corrinne says that to make it feel like Christmas, she's going to spend the holiday with Randy and Chloe. This, she says, is being done for Chloe's sake. The child gives Arnie a Christmas card before going off with her mother. Becker realizes how desperately he wants to spend the holidays with them, which is surprising even to him.

Markowitz is meeting with a client when Ann Kelsey barges in and announces that it's time for them to go to the hospital. Stuart gets all flustered but does manage to get them to the hospital in one piece. Kelsey goes through 20 hours of labor and gives birth to a healthy baby boy.

The penalty phase of the Earl Williams case is under way. Margaret Flanagan puts Nina Corry's sister Nicole on the stand, and the woman testifies that she remembers a time Nina said she was afraid of Williams. Next, Flanagan is given permission by the judge to show the jury explicit photographs of Nina's bludgeoned body. Kuzak grows more frustrated, feeling his case is slipping through his fingers. In an effort to counter this damage, he puts Williams' mother on the stand, and the woman

pleads with the jury not to take her son's life. Dr. Parks testifies that Williams does not deserve the death penalty. Flanagan gets Parks to admit he is so opposed to the death penalty, he would reject it being used against *any* person, no matter how severe the crime.

Despite the man's testimony being rejected earlier, Kuzak calls Phillip Holden to the stand. Judge Harbin rejects the witness and tells Kuzak that she will bring him up on charges. Summations are given, the jury deliberates and the verdict is read: Earl Williams is sentenced to die.

Episode Sixty-Nine

"The Good Human Bar"

Rollins is approached by law school friend Paula Lights, who has an inoperable brain tumor and wants to take a crack at her one last chance at life: cryonics. She will have her head removed from her body and frozen until the day that a cure is found, then she will be revived. Naturally she recognizes the implausibility of such a thing, but if there's even a chance that she can live again, she wants to take it. Reluctantly, Rollins takes on the case and goes to court.

The state feels this is suicide and Judge Conover looks at it as Rollins seeking permission from the court to allow euthanasia. Rollins brings cryogenic expert Dr. Raymond Simon to the stand, and he testifies it is conceivable that such a cure will one day be found and that this method will pay off. State lawyer Keene argues that the whole idea of what they're talking about is laughable and his witness, Dr. Wayland Lettora, testifies that cryogenics is socially irresponsible.

Paula is given an opportunity to speak for herself, and Judge Conover is so moved by her words that he rules in her favor, knowing full well that it will be appealed by the state. In fact, Keene wants to file an appeal at that moment, but Conover won't accept it until the following day. What he essentially has done is give Paula 24 hours to do what she wants to do. She and Rollins have dinner and she departs, leaving her devastated friend behind.

(NOTE: The pleasant thing about this story line is that it gives Blair Underwood the opportunity to portray Jonathan Rollins in a court scene where there is something more personal at stake. Gone is the grandstanding lawyer we're used to seeing. In his place is a more down-to-earth attorney who is as equally appealing.)

Becker is asked by attorney Sheldon Ganz to join him in their own matrimonial practice, and Arnie has to give this serious thought. He asks Roxanne if she would go with him if he left. Despite being shocked at the question, Roxanne says that she would. Meanwhile, Roxanne has been taking singing and dancing lessons to build her confidence so she can perform at a local club's amateur night. Kuzak hits it off with Rox's instructor, Kimberly Dugan, who is teaching her and another woman in the firm's file room how to move. On the night of the big show, Roxanne goes up in front of the crowd and is struck by stage fright. Markowitz and Abby, who are standing in the wings, come out, join her, instill confidence and depart as Roxanne brings the song home.

Sifuentes gets a phone call telling him Allison has been raped by one of the actors in a commercial she's directing. Sifuentes takes her to a police line-up where she picks Henrico Mores out and in the hallway Victor almost strangles the man before three police officers pull him off. As Allison explains it, Henrico gave her a ride home, came in for a cup of coffee and raped her. Sifuentes tries to talk to her about this,

but she doesn't want to, feeling fearful and blaming herself. Next day, he goes to see Van Owen and asks her to take on the case, which she agrees to do. Sifuentes warns Allison that Henrico's attorney will try to attack her, making her the criminal. Although fearful of this, Allison will go forward with the trial.

Episode Seventy

"Noah's Bark"

Written by David E. Kelley and William M. Finkelstein

Directed by Win Phelps

Guest Stars: Jackie Gayle (Sol Rosen), Jill Vance (Secretary), Joyce Hyser (Allison Gottlieb), Michael Russo (Henrico Mores), Olivia Cole (Judge Julia McFarlane), Ed Krieger (Clerk— Judge MacFarlane), Bruce Fairbairn (Sheldon Ganz), Stanley Grover (Judge Richard Lobel), Lora Staley (Lisa Maynard), Victoria Dakil (Foreperson), Lenny Wolpe (Noah Cowan), Ann Marie Lee (Susan Jenkins), Terry Kiser (Sal Cassella), Bill Gratton (Judge Steven Greg), Peter Schuck (Dr. Herbert Towel), Deborah May (Carla Stritch)

Van Owen puts Allison on the stand in a preliminary hearing to detail the night of the rape. Henrico's attorney, Susan Jenkins, moves in for the kill, trying to prove that Allison acted in a flirtatious way with Henrico, and that in the past she has had affairs with two other members of her crew. Sifuentes is called next, and is hit with questions about his personal and sexual relationship with Allison. Van Owen continues to argue the point, and the judge agrees there is enough probable cause to warrant a trial.

Jenkins comes to her with a plea bargain: felony assault, with four years in prison and two on parole. Otherwise, and only if the jury finds Henrico guilty, he will be sentenced to three years, with a likely release coming after a year and a half. Considering this, Allison says she will go for the former, but changes her mind at the last minute. Henrico raped her, and he deserves to be punished as a rapist. Later, Van Owen tells Allison that a woman watching coverage of the trial on TV has stepped forward, admitting that Henrico raped her as well.

Becker and Roxanne raid the files of McKenzie-Brackman in the middle of the night and leave. During the staff meeting, where everyone notices his absence, Brackman receives a telegram from Becker which says he has resigned from the firm. McKenzie is angry and asks all the partners to meet him that evening. During that meeting, the thought arises that Becker might have stolen clients, and to this end Rosalind suggests they get a restraining order. In other words, the firm might not have those clients, but neither would Arnie Becker.

Next day, McKenzie and Kuzak meet with Becker and Ganz and Judge Hale, who grants the restraining order filed by the firm. At the office in private, Becker tells McKenzie that he felt betrayed by the firm in the video lawsuit, he doesn't like the idea that Rosalind has a superior position to him and that McKenzie always seems to treat Kuzak more favorably. Sounding like a father talking to an unhappy offspring, McKenzie asks Becker what he wants. The response: his name added to the firm's title, because it will provide a greater emotional connection. McKenzie agrees.

Rollins handles the case of Noah Cowan, a sufferer of Tourette's Syndrome, a neurological disorder that results in all kinds of twitches and the involuntary unleashing of degrading remarks to people, even though the man doesn't mean these things. Noah recently was fired from his market research job, because he was in-advertently insulting people and no one wants to work with him. Dr. Towel, who also suffers from the disease, is called to the stand by Rollins, and he testifies that he is able to function in society and there's no reason Noah can't as well. Carla Stritch, the defense attorney, counters that Towel is testifying as a victim of the disease, not an expert.

Noah's former boss, Sal Cassela, is forced to admit that he fired Noah because of the handicap, noting that the man's work was always excellent. Noah is awarded $250,000 by the jury. Cassela approaches Noah and suggests an alternative: $50,000, a new car and his job back plus a promotion. The only difference is that he will work at home utilizing a FAX machine. Rollins is against the idea, but Noah, aware that Cassela really wants him and that the world would be biased to him anyway, is happy to accept.

Episode Seventy-One

"The Pay's Lousy, But the Tips Are Great"

Written by William M. Finkelstein and David E. Kelley

Directed by David Carson

Guest Stars: Joyce Hyser (Allison Gottlieb), Keith Mills (Judge Water Green), Nehemiah Persoff (Isadore Glickman), Raymond Singer (Ralph King), Paul Mantee (Judge Mitchell Katlin), Alan Feinstein (Judge Henry Sawyer), Bob Ross (Clerk), Ken Zavayna (Foreperson), Natalia Nogulich (Helen Keris), Brenda Hillhouse (Caroline Speck), Hansford Rowe (Daniel Siegfried), Kim Myers (Kerry Martin), Robert Levine (Benjamin Claflin), Tom Henschel (Bruce Gorosh)

Sifuentes represents Kerry Martin, a woman recently fired by Judge Henry Sawyer because they had been having an affair and he no longer wants to jeopardize his marriage. Sifuentes argues for Kerry that such an abrupt firing would have an adverse effect on her career. Sawyer admits to everything, but Sifuentes argues that he made her a victim for something that wasn't even her fault. Opposing counsel states that Kerry is making more money at her current law firm job than she had with Sawyer, but Sifuentes counters that she went through emotional scarring and diminished self-esteem from being fired.

The jury awards her $15,000 in compensatory damages and $250,000 in punitive damages. Victory ringing in his ears, Sifuentes buys flowers and head home to Allison, but she is packed up and ready to leave. They haven't been getting along as of late, she's trying to recover mentally from the rape and somehow she gets the feeling that Sifuentes blames her. Maybe they'll get together again some day, but it isn't likely. Victor reminds her of that day and the pain she feels.

(NOTE: Allison Gottlieb was the longest relationship we've seen Victor involved in to date. It really seemed that this was going to be the *girl for him. Unfortunately, it didn't last and now he's a free agent again.)*

Everyone is giving Becker and Roxanne the silent treatment, angry that he tried to sneak out the way he did. Even Benny is nasty, and this results in a confrontation where Arnie chastises him for being rude, when he's always there for him. Later, Benny apologizes.

Markowitz is sent back to trial, this time representing the elderly Rabbi Isadore Glickman, who nicked the penis of a child during a circumcision. Now the father, Bruce Gorosh, is demanding damages for permanent disfigurement that will haunt the boy some day.

Markowitz lays out the perfect argument: the child will live his life as an orthodox Jew, so he will not have sex before he is married and the woman he marries will also be an orthodox Jew and therefore a virgin. The end result is she will have nothing to compare the boy's penis to. Rabbi Glickman is nonetheless found guilty and Gorosh is awarded $40,000. Added to this is the fact that Glickman is prohibited from performing any more circumcisions, because the next time it might not be only a nick.

Rosalind Shays, who some may dramatically equate with Damien or Rosemary's baby, puts her games of manipulation into action, all designed to solidify her own base of power. One of the firm's biggest clients, Feldenkranz, is thinking of leaving. Rosalind convinces McKenzie and Brackman to let her meet with him on her own. Alone with CEO Dan Siegfried, she basically puts down McKenzie's competence ("That's why they brought me in," she says), and promises that if Feldenkranz remains with McKenzie-Brackman, she will personally handle his account. If he's not completely satisfied with her work after 90 days, then he's free to leave. He considers this for a moment, and agrees.

Back at the office, she tells Brackman that she was able to keep the account, but Siegfried laid out the condition that she must personally handle the account. Obviously this is a touchy situation, as Leland had been their lawyer. Brackman tells her not to worry about it; that he'll speak to McKenzie for her. This takes place and McKenzie then thanks her for keeping the account.

Rosalind takes that moment to mention that she has a $5 million a year client she used to represent willing to swing over to the firm. The only problem is that it is a competitor to one of Brackman's clients which brings in about $100,000 per year. McKenzie says he'll discuss the matter with Brackman. Rosalind thanks him and leaves. There's a wonderful shot of McKenzie

125

as she leaves. His expression betrays the fact that he doesn't trust her for a second.

(NOTE: To many, Rosalind Shays may seem like the quintessential bitch and those people may wonder why a character like her was added. Frankly, a show like L.A. Law *needs someone like Rosalind to mix things up a bit; to keep everybody on their toes and to create better, more realistic drama. Already the groundwork is being laid down for what is yet to come.)*

Episode Seventy-Two

"True Brit"

Written by William M. Finkelstein and David E. Kelley

Directed by Arthur Allan Seidelman

Guest Stars: Christopher Neame (Alan Scott), John Standing (Nigel Morris), Courtney Thorne-Smith (Kimberly Dugan), Jennifer Hetrick (Corrinne Hammond), Larry Dobkin (Judge Saul Edelstein), Renee Jones (Diana Moses), Drew Snyder (Bernard Lavelle), Britt Leach (Walter Brown), Howard Mungo (Detective #2), John O'Connell (Robert Davies), Paul Lyell (Detective #1), Nomi Mitty (Marion Davies), Kay Douglas (Waitress), Stan Kamber (Judge Harlan Shubow), Jeff Kizer (Manny Jackson), Cedering Fox (Anchorwoman), Gus Corrado (Foreperson), Jay Ingram (John Siltan)

Kuzak comes up against English barrister sir Nigel Morris, who comes across as the perfect English gentleman in the courtroom, but a ruthless, cold-hearted rat in private. The case involves Walt Brown (Kuzak's client), an American businessman who is suing Alan Scott, an English candy maker who runs his own conglomerate. A deal entered into in good faith is driving Brown out of business.

The idea was that Brown would supply a specialized candy for Scott to distribute in Canada, but Scott has been importing the candy to America at a lower cost than Brown charges in America, therefore he can't compete with his own product. Sir Nigel argues that this is what American business is all about, but the jury finds in favor of Walt Brown.

Becker is still getting the cold shoulder from everyone. He's feeling totally disgusted and even talks to Kuzak about it. Kuzak argues that obviously people wanted him back, but Becker says it was the clients the partners were interested in, not Arnold Becker. Arnie also wants to know what happened to the friendship he and Kuzak once had. They used to do things together, hang out and be very close. Now, as they've gotten older, they've lost that. Kuzak understands what he's saying, and at a later point in the episode we see them on a double date. Also happening is a surprise party to welcome Arnie as a partner. Apparently all has been forgiven.

Rosalind and Abby meet with new client Bernard Lavelle, who questions Abby's competency as his legal representative. Abby storms out of the room, leaving Rosalind to tell Lavelle that if Abby isn't good enough for him, then he can take his business elsewhere. Shocked by the vehement support, he agrees. Rosalind next goes to Abby and tells her what transpired, adding that Abby also made a mistake: voice your feelings, but *never* walk out on a client. Two points for Ros!

Motherhood is wonderful, but Ann Kelsey is really missing the office. She phases back into the work routine and enter her office to find Rosalind sitting behind her desk, with permission from Markowitz. Kelsey immediately starts snapping that Rosalind should hang up the phone and get out from behind her desk. Rosalind does so and tries an apology but Ann is ice. Markowitz comes in and gets his head handed to him for having given Rosalind permission to use the office while her own was being painted.

(NOTE: It's understandable that Ann Kelsey could feel that something isn't right about Rosalind. The amazing thing is that she often refers to Rosalind as the "Queen Bitch," but in these scenes she does quite nicely by that title herself.)

Rollins is approached by Diana Moses, who tells him that her friend Manny hit a boy on a bike while driving 50 miles per hour and then drove away. Manny didn't report the accident because of the fear of going to prison. The boy is dead, off the main road. When she asks if there's anything that can be done, Rollins goes to McKenzie and Sifuentes and is told that to inform the police or the boy's parents would be a betrayal of the attorney/client privilege, and that is something that simply cannot be violated.

Rollins and Diana go to the scene of the accident without telling anyone, and find the body. Rollins checks the boy's pulse only to find that he is dead. Not knowing what else to do, Rollins goes to Van Owen and tells her what has transpired, hoping that Manny will be able to get complete immunity. Van Owen can't cut such a deal, and to make matters worse, now she is a district attorney who is aware of a lawyer who knows where a missing body is. As a result, Rollins is arrested for interfering in the investigation of a murder.

Rollins is brought in for arraignment and Van Owen asks Judge Shubow to waive the attorney/client privilege, which the man simply will not do. As Rollins, who is now free, leaves the courtroom, he is approached by the parents of the missing child. They are stunned by the judge's decision. Sifuentes turns to Van Owen and snaps, "Did you arrange this too, Grace?" She takes offense to the charge. Rollins is hustled out of the courtroom by Sifuentes.

That night, Rollins is with Diana Moses when the doorbell rings. He opens it to find the boy's parents there, tearfully asking him yet again to tell them where their little boy is. He can't say anything, and slowly closes the door.

(NOTE: This Jonathan Rollins story is probably one of the best the character has been given to date. His moral decisions are gut-wrenching and his frustration of not knowing who to turn to is tangible. Van Owen's choices are also tough, though you can't help but be angry at her for doing what she does to Jonathan. Finally, the emotions of the parents are incredible. The level of pain of not knowing where your child is, while someone else does but can't say anything, is almost too much to bear.)

Episode Seventy-Three

"On Your Honor"

Written by David E. Kelley, William M. Finkelstein and Cynthia Saunders

Directed Steve Robman

Guest Stars: Mimi Lieber (Sherri Fajed), Reid Shelton (Judge Nelson Aldrich), Steven Gilborn (Robert Richards), Courtney Thorne-Smith (Kimberly Dugan), James Harper (Michael Stoner), James Avery (Judge Michael Conover), Bruce Kirby (D.A. Bruce Rogoff), Mark Robman (Ada Halpern), David Proval (William Mayer), James O'Sullivan (Steven Stirling), Anthony DeFonte (Don Seidel), Douglas Roberts (Richard Yzerman), Tracy Justrich (Valley Girl), Susan Krebs (Nancy Anderson), Reid Smith (Douglas Wittenberg), Beth Taylor (Denise), Ellen Blake (Elizabeth Brand), Biff Wiff (Clerk), Jill Vance (Holly), Robin Pearson Rose (Ada Peters), Mark Klastorin (Ada Haller), Richard Zavaglia

(Yonker), John Witherspoon (Mark Steadman), Deenie Dakota (Valley Girl), Roger Nolan (Ada Bill Gros), Rif Hutton (Ada Jenkins)

Roxanne leads the other secretaries in strike when Brackman cracks down on them too hard by instituting staggered lunch hours, trying to stop talking among them as a waste of time and money and refusing to give them a raise. Brackman will not back down from his demands and Roxanne follows through with her threat. Things backfire, however, when the women learn that they have been fired.

Roxanne, who is in a different financial situation than the rest of them, as Arnie Becker points out to her, meets with Brackman to negotiate. He will drop the staggered lunch hours and agrees not to put up dividers between the secretaries. But due to the unstable financial situation at the term, raises at this time are out of the question. Roxanne agrees, as do the other secretaries.

Following the death of Judge Rainbow, Van Owen is asked to take his place on the bench. She's nervous, but ultimately agrees. Both apprehensive and excited, she rushes to tell Kuzak, but is surprised to find Kimberly Dugan there, modeling her new Laker Girl uniform for him. The following day she begins her new life as a judge and it is as chaotic a first day as one can find. As things progress, she is shocked when an assistant district attorney recommends a life sentence for a 16-year-old boy convicted in the drive-by shooting of two people.

Calling a recess, she goes to see Judge Conover for advice. He offers two thoughts: first, consider the kind of world you want to live in and, second, don't let anyone in your courtroom read indecision on your face. She sleeps on these words, and the following day stuns everyone by sentencing the 16-year-old to life im-

prisonment. Later, Kuzak comes to see her to provide his congratulations, and hands her a wooden gavel.

She is truly grateful, noting that even though they're no longer together, he's still the one she thinks of running to when something exciting happens. He feels the same way, and the two of them embrace and begin making love, the passion of the moment getting the best of them.

Sifuentes' client is Sherri Fajed, an Iranian woman whose husband was on a commercial airliner shot down by the U.S. Navy as a hostile aircraft. U.S. Attorney General Robert Richards thinks the entire case should be thrown out of court, because what happened, as tragic as it was, was a matter of foreign policy, not something that should be dealt with in the courts. It is the opinion of the Navy's assistant secretary, Michael Stoner, that such a litigation might jeopardize national security, which is a risk they dare not take. It is Sifuentes' argument that the Navy was negligent in shooting down the plane.

During a private moment, the government offers to settle for $250,000, but Sherri wants to continue. She wants the world to know what happened. Surprisingly, the lawsuit is not dismissed by the court system. Back at the office, Rosalind puts pressure on McKenzie about Victor's case. Going to him, Leland explains that Sifuentes should drop Sherri's case because one of the firm's major clients has placed a bid on a very large defense contract, and such a lawsuit—one represented by McKenzie-Brackman's involvement—could threaten it.

Sifuentes can't believe his ears. He is furious and tells McKenzie categorically that he will not withdraw from this case. Sifuentes goes back to court to continue his battle, but Sherri tells him that she's going to drop the lawsuit and accept the government's settlement offer due to the fact that the INS has gotten hold of her phone records and the fear is very much alive in her that she will be deported. Without her husband she is lost, but $250,000 will at least help build a life for herself in America.

Episode Seventy-Four

"Whatever Happened to Hannah?"

Written by Christopher Keyser and Amy Lippman

Directed by Tom Moore

Guest Stars: David Paymer (Joey Paul), Sue Giosa (Lainie Paul), Courtney-Thorne Smith (Kimberly Dugan), Raye Birk (Judge Steven Lang), Lillian Lehman (Judge Mary Harcourt), Lee Kessler (Frieda Sitkowitz), Momo Yashimo (Foreperson), Paul Regina (Felix Echeverria), Peter Michael Goetz (Dr. Robert Woolf), Sian Barbara Allen (Diane Campbell), Edward Edwards (John Campbell), Brecklin Meyer (Brian Campbell)

The war between Kelsey and Rosalind heats up, beginning with Kelsey asking Rosalind to get out of her chair at the staff meeting and then wanting to take over a case that Rosalind has invested a month of her time in. Kelsey argues that this is her client and now she's ready to fill the void of her absence and carry her share. "I sensed no void," is Rosalind's cool response. The barbs fly, with Rosalind saying this particular client wants her to represent him and that's the end of it. Both women issue warnings not to take the other on. Then Rosalind plays poor victim to McKenzie, who goes to talk to Kelsey.

Kuzak and Van Owen both agree that their lovemaking session was a one-time thing and that's it. For the next few days he's distant from Kimberly, but eventually tells her that he wants her to be a part of his life.

Rollins represents stand-up comic Joey Paul, who claims his ex-wife/partner has been heckling him at his nightclub performances, destroying his act and making it much more difficult for him to get gigs. Lainie Paul, on the other hand, is counter-suing, claiming Joey is using her material in his show without permission and she wants it stopped. The two of them constantly insult each other in the courtroom and are told to stop by the judge.

Joey comes up with what he considers to be a brainstorm: he'll perform his own material in the courtroom and let the jury decide if he's funny or not. As unorthodox as this is, the judge allows it. Joey performs and bombs horribly. Lainie actually has a look of pity on her face. The lawyers try to work out a settlement, but Rollins is surprised to see Joey and Lainie talking to each other civilly, with her offering advice on his career. The two leave for a cup of coffee.

Abby represents Diane Campbell, who, for years was abused by her ex-husband John and has not been able to enjoy a normal physical or emotional relationship since they broke up. John's lawyer, Felix Echeverria, sets out to prove that Diane made John think she actually liked to get beat up, because very often they would make love right afterwards. Abby is totally turned off by this line of questioning, and objects as often as possible, at one point saying, "Permission to vomit, your honor?"

Echeverria's biggest argument is that Diane simply should have left the marriage, but she didn't. Why? According to him, it's because she needed the abuse; it made her feel wanted. Abby focuses on the fear of abuse, how it makes you too afraid to try to do anything about it. *Now* Diane is trying to take a stand for herself. The jury deliberates on this issue and comes back with a guilty verdict for John, but they only award Diane $1,500.

129

Diane thanks Abby for everything she tried to do and mentions the fact that she is going out with John for a cup of coffee so they can talk things over. Abby tells her that she's making the biggest mistake of her life; that if she goes for the coffee it will only be the first step back into the hell she's trying to get out of. Diane considers this and breaks the date with John, asking Abby if she's free for dinner, which she is.

Episode Seventy-Five

"Ex-Wives and Video Tape"

Written by David E. Kelley and William M. Finkelstein

Directed by Miles Watkins

Guest Stars: Renee Jones (Diana Moses), Veronica Cartwright (Margaret Flanagan), Courtney Thorne-Smith (Kimberly Dugan), Carl Lumbly (Earl Williams), Vonetta McGee (Jackie Williams), Andy Romano (Barney Dowe), Lorinne Vozoff (Judge Roberta Harbin), Donald Hotton (Supreme Court Judge Richardskull), Mort Sertner (Supreme Court Judge Donald Tytell), Norman Bartold (Supreme Court Judge Connolly), Kate Randolph Burns (Clerk), Biff Wiff (Clerk), Parley Baer (Supreme Court Judge Parker), Randy Kovitz (Kevin Zachary), Patience Cleveland (Supreme Court Justice Washington), Tina Panella-Hart (Reporter #1), Erin Gray (Rochelle Peters), Vic Polizos (Al Vogel), Jeffrey Josephson (Johnny Kayle), Steve Tietsort (Reporter)

Rollins gets his ire up when Rosalind brings aboard Anderson Industries, a company that has investment ties to South Africa. He has serious problems being associated with a law firm that would allow such clients in, as he discusses with McKenzie. Leland promises to bring the issue up to the other partners, which he does. It looks as though Rollins' feelings have real sup-

port, until Rosalind starts declaring her outrage of company policy being dictated by an associate.

A ballot is taken and McKenzie is left with the deciding vote. He considers the needs of the firm—or he's trying avoid a battle—and votes yes. Rollins is told of this and says that he's thinking about quitting. Later, he talks to Diana Moses about it and assumes that she'll quit to, but she refuses to. Just because they're black, it doesn't mean they have to take on the responsibility of the world. What difference would their quitting make to the situation in South Africa? Rollins has to admit that her words make sense.

At episode's end, McKenzie decides that he's going to officially change his vote. Anderson Industries will *not* be represented by McKenzie-Brackman. Rosalind is beside herself, stating that McKenzie is unwilling to make a hard decision because he's afraid of losing his popularity.

Becker represents Al Vogel, who is threatening to sell a video tape of his wife to an adult video company. She is now a famous television anchorwoman and on this tape is footage of her having sex with him and trying all kinds of "kinky" things. Her network tries to negotiate the tape away, but Al keeps raising the price. Finally it comes down to his ex-wife, Rochelle Peters, talking to him directly to find out why he would do such a thing. What spurred him on was being referred to as "my friend, Al Vogel," rather than her husband.

Rochelle decides not to fight him. If he wants to release the tape, he can. All it will prove to the world is that she loved her husband and he was a sleazy little man who tried to profit from it. Al breaks down and says that he wants to be her husband again, but Rochelle sympathetically tells him that that's not going to happen. Becker, as hard as it may be to believe, is the one who talks Al out of releasing the tape.

(NOTE: Erin Gray (Rochelle Peters) is well known to television viewers for her co-stars roles in such series as Buck Rogers, Silver Spoons *and the extremely short-lived* E.A.R.T.H. Force.*)*

Kuzak files a death penalty appeal for Earl Williams before the Supreme Court, noting the prosecutorial misconduct of Margaret Flanagan. She didn't notify him of DNA evidence prior to the trial as she was supposed to. The group of judges consider this and actually rule in Kuzak's favor (a first in this trial), saying the unexpected DNA evidence did indeed prevent Earl Williams from getting a fair trial. A new trial is ordered immediately, and Kuzak lets out a huge sigh of relief. The one suspect in the case he has is Ronald Sewell, who he can't have the police pick up. Instead, he has a couple of fierce looking "gentlemen" find him and arrange a meeting.

Episode Seventy-Six

"Blood, Sweat & Tears"

Written by David E. Kelley

Directed by Edwin Sherin

Guest Stars: Veronica Cartwright (Margaret Flanagan), Beah Richards (Alberta Williams), Carl Lumbly (Earl Williams), Vonetta McGee (Jackie Williams), Stanley Kamel (Mark Gilliam), Franc Luz (Dr. Michael Dayan), Christine Estabrook (Susan Parral), Andrea Covell (Foreperson), Warren Munson (Judge Matthew Saucier), John Carter (Dr. John Petit), Lorinne Vozoff (Judge Roberta Harbin), Jeffrey Josephson (Johnny Kayle), Bill Feeney (Guard), Kate Randolph Burns (Clerk—Harbin), Stewart Wilson-Turner (Earl Williams, Jr.), Dayna Winston (Janine Williams), Mimi Cagnetta (Secretary), George Buck (Les Corry), Leon (Pinto)

Tired of all the fighting that has been going on of late, McKenzie announces he is stepping down as senior partner. After getting over the initial shock of this announcement, the three people most interested in wanting to be the new senior partner are Brackman, Markowitz and Rosalind. A vote is taken and Rosalind Shays turns out to be the winner. In private, McKenzie consults with Brackman, stating he voted for him as did Becker and Kuzak. Douglas Brackman cast the deciding vote for Rosalind, believing that he would never get elected and that the firm would be better off in Rosalind's hands than those of Markowitz.

Sifuentes represents surgeon Michael Dayan, who refused to operate on a patient because the man had AIDS and he was afraid of contracting the disease. Now the dead man's wife, Susan Parral, is suing for wrongful death. Sifuentes argues that Michael Parral had only a few months to live and that Dayan knew this, which played a part in his reasoning. In recess, Sifuentes offers a settlement deal of $75,000, but opposing counsel Mark Gilliam refuses the offer.

When court is back in session, Gilliam calls Dr. John Petit to the stand and he testifies that what Dayan did goes against everything being a doctor stands for. If this is the case, Sifuentes muses, then why hasn't Dayan been brought up on disciplinary action by the American Medical Association or the hospital? Why is he still practicing medicine?

Gilliam, who we eventually learn also is dying of AIDS, presents an eloquent closing argument, emphasizing that as a man who knew his life would end in about 90 days, Dayan was grateful for every moment he had to live. Each moment was a glorious thing to be cherished, and when he woke up every morning the whole thing could start again. By not operating on him, Dayan denied what was left to him—what he deserved to have. These words obviously touch the jury, as they find in favor of Susan Parral and award her $250,000.

Kuzak meets with Ronald Sewell, his one suspect in the Earl Williams case, who was found by private investigators. Kuzak starts to question him and is stunned to learn that Sewell already had been questioned by Margaret Flanagan, a fact that never came to light during the trial. Although he's a hostile witness, Sewell goes before Judge Harbin and tells her that Flanagan had indeed questioned him regarding the Nina Corry death. Harbin turns to Flanagan and, for the first time, lashes into her for such inappropriate behavior. The next day, Harbin puts both lawyers in their place for their tactics during this trial and then dismisses the charges against Earl Williams. He is once again a free man.

(NOTE: And now the audience as well as Michael Kuzak can take a moment and relax from this long but riveting trial. Given the twists and turns that sometimes occur in episodes of the series, it would almost be expected that within the next few episodes Earl Williams would end up arrested again, once more charged with murder. This did not happen, but one has to wonder if he is guilty of the crime. True that Kuzak got the case thrown out of court, but that was based more on a technicality than anything else. It's an interesting question mark that, to date, has not been addressed.)

Episode Seventy-Seven

"Bound For Glory"

Written by David E. Kelley and William M. Finkelstein

Directed by Win Phelps

Guest Stars: Richard Venture (Abe Lassen), Dan Hedaya (Michael Roit-man), George Dickerson (Joseph Haas), Alan Rosenberg (Clinton Willis), Zoaunne Leroy (Gretchen Wynn), Dick Anthony Williams (Charles Jackson), Andrew Hill Newman (Jerry Svetka), Richard Zavaglia (Yonker), Tina Chappen (Foreperson), Mark Klastorin (Ada Haller), Don Davis (Judge Richard Batke), Michael DeLuise (Keith Haas), Floyd Foster, Jr. (Clerk), Richard Marcus (Ray Breecher), Keith Mills (Judge Walter Green), Bill Mondy (Paul Zweibel), Peter Kevoian (D.A. Jim Aoli), Judith Jordan (Pauline Haas), Kisha Oglesby (Faith Jackson), Zeljko Ivanek (Joel Lassen), Ed Williams (Ed Tobias)

Rollins is representing country fair packager Gretchen Wynn, who's being sued by Ray Breecher. The man claims he was disqualified from entering his frog in a frog-jumping contest because of the size of his web-footed friend. Actually it's not surprising when one sees this creature. It may resemble a frog, but is extremely large, able to leap 30 feet at a time. Ultimately the judge rules that, despite its enormous size, it's still a frog and should not have been disqualified. Breecher is awarded $150,000.

As a favor to Benny, Markowitz offers to help him settle an argument with a friend he offered to sell some baseball cards to. Now the man is claiming that Benny is not selling him all the cards, which Benny maintains was never his intention. Yes, he wanted to raise some money for his upcoming marriage to Alice, but he would never part with all his cards. Unfortunately, as the legal machine gets involved, the whole situation grows more complex. Finally, Benny and his friend decide to work it out between themselves without any lawyers.

Abby's client is Joel Lasson, son of a McKenzie-Brackman client, who has been arrested for the third time on drug possession charges. Abby is convinced

Richard Dysart portrays paternalistic founding partner Leland McKenzie, a principled, compassionate man in the competitive, cutthroat legal jungle.

Alan Rachins portrays Douglas Brackman, the unrelentingly compulsive managing partner.

that Joel can be gotten off on probation, but his father, Abe, actually wants him to go to jail for six months as it seems to be the only way the youth will clean up his act. As Abe is Becker's client, he supports the man's decision. Brackman agrees. At a preliminary hearing, the District Attorney asks for a guilty plea and probation. Abby accepts this and Abe demands the firm fire her. Becker and Brackman attack Abby, but Rosalind stands up for her because her client was Joel Lasson, not *Abe* Lasson.

Kelsey goes before Judge Van Owen with the case of the Jacksons, a black family whose son was kicked to death by the skinhead son, Carl, of Mr. and Mrs. Haas. The Jacksons are suing for parental liability in their son's death. It is Kelsey's intention to prove to the jury that the Mr. and Mrs. Haas did nothing to prevent their son's bigotry. She puts Carl on the stand, and he tells how they never stopped him from doing what he wanted to do. Mr. Haas apologizes profusely to the Jacksons, while stating to the jury that they may not have stopped Carl's bigotry, but they weren't responsible for it and never thought that it would end in someone's death.

Kelsey declares this hatred was born at home and was nurtured in the soul of Carl Haas. If something isn't done about it in this courtroom, that kind of bigotry will continue to thrive in the world. Van Owen points out to the jury that they are to deliberate over the propensity of violence, not how a family shapes the mind of their children. In private, Kelsey is angry at these instructions, believing that Van Owen has almost guaranteed a "not guilty" verdict. Grace stops the conversation at that point, saying that friendship or not, she will hold Kelsey in contempt. The jury comes in and, surprisingly, finds the Haas' liable and awards the Jacksons $150,000 in damages.

(If nothing else, this moving case presents a very different view of Grace Van Owen and a member of McKenzie-Brackman. For the first time we see her "pulling rank," and the frustration Kelsey feels at being friends with someone who has become a judge. It should be said that Jill Eikenberry does a great job in this trial, vividly driving home her point, because it would seem that such racial intolerance would indeed be born in the home.)

Episode Seventy-Eight

"Justice Swerved"

Written by David E. Kelley and Bryce Zabel

Directed by Menachem Binetski

Guest Stars: Bruce Ornstein (John Trischuta), Earl Boen (Judge Walter L. Swanson), Jordan Baker (D.A. Marcia Cortwright), Pamela Roberts (Clerk), Ethan Phillips (Dr. Sam Waibel), Mary Gregory (Judge R.A. Pendleton), John Frederick Jones (John Williams), Elena Stiteler (Ada Ellen Harris), William Converse-Roberts (Wayne Lafferty), Joan McMurtrey (Elizabeth Lafferty), Robyn Peterson (Marilyn Hopkins), Richard Grove (Officer Pratt), Richard Dunn (Cop #1), Kelly R. Kleinman (ND Officer), Lita Stevens (Foreperson), Virgil Wilson (Cop #3), Tina Panella-Hart (Reporter #1), Orin Kennedy (Reporter #2), Cal Gibson (Reporter #3), Cheryl Carter (Desk Sergeant), Don Pugsley (Davis), Peter Jolly (Clerk #2)

Brackman is having problems with his sex life, which he attributes to guilt over his failed marriage. McKenzie relates a story of a similar problem involving his relationship with Jennifer, and a sex therapist he saw that cured it. Feeling he has nothing to lose, Brackman decides to give it a try and meets with Marilyn Hopkins. She is a surrogate partner who helps men overcome their sexual hang-ups and problems. Several sessions pass with them connecting emotionally and mentally, and then she wants to try something physical. They take off their clothes. Marilyn kisses Brackman gently on the lips and then kisses him a second time. Brackman rolls his eyes, passes wind and collapses to the ground. And yes, dear readers, this is the first time that sound has been heard on network television.

Following lunch at a fancy restaurant, Kelsey and Markowitz decide to stop at a hotel to make love. Markowitz, who has had a couple of glasses of wine, runs a red light and is pulled over by the police. He is arrested for DWI and charged. Kuzak pulls some strings and works it out so no charges are pressed. Kelsey is overjoyed, but Markowitz isn't. He feels as though he could have hurt someone seriously by not being completely with it, but because he knows people in the right places, he got away with a crime. There is no satisfaction in this victory.

Sifuentes and lawyer John Trischuta represent Elizabeth and Wayne Lafferty, charged with murdering their newborn son. While Dr. Sam Weibel says his examination indicates child abuse, Sifuentes argues that the child fell victim to Sudden Infant Death Syndrome (SIDS), a disease often misdiagnosed as suffocation. The bruises on the child's body, he adds, came from attempts at resuscitation, which usually happens in such cases.

The D.A.'s argument is that Wayne wanted the child dead because it was born blind with intestinal problems, and that raising a child with such conditions would create a financial hardship. There are witnesses who claim Wayne said he wished the child would die just to be put out of its misery. They also learn the man had tried to put the child up for adoption, but was unable to do so, which he was told the

day before his son's death. This is a revelation to both Sifuentes and Trischuta.

That night, Elizabeth comes to Sifuentes to detail her feelings. She doesn't want to suspect her husband, but she found an article on SIDS in the man's desk, with details on bruises highlighted. Sifuentes wants her to come forward with this information, and she agrees, albeit reluctantly. Next day, both Wayne and Trischuta are shocked by what she says. When Wayne gets up on the stand, he says his wife is actually guilty of the murder. To support this, he cites such things as her extreme depression after the child's birth and her acting strangely on the night of his death. At trial's end, Sifuentes and Trischuta argue that their respective client is innocent while the other is guilty.

The D.A. argues that this is all an act, that the couple are trying to create reasonable doubt on the part of the jury so that these parents who murdered their baby will go free. If so, it works, because the jury finds them not guilty. Afterwards, the Laffertys, Sifuentes, Trischuta and other people silently get into the elevator. Wayne and Elizabeth don't say a word to each other, but they briefly squeeze each other's hands. Sifuentes sees this and slumps backwards, shocked at the way both he and Trischuta were manipulated. To make matters worse, the Laffertys cannot be tried again due to the "Double Jeopardy" law.

(NOTE: One heck of a story, and Jimmy Smits, who won the Emmy for best actor in a dramatic series, is just incredible. The emotion and wonderful acting that goes on in that final scene in the elevator must be viewed to be believed. He says so much with his eyes and facial expression, and the audience is left with its collective mouth hanging open as well. This is the kind of thing that separates L.A. Law *from so many*

other series.)

Episode Seventy-Nine

"Watts A Matter?"

Written by David E. Kelley and Bryce Zabel

Directed by Tom Moore

Guest Stars: Humberto Ortiz (Felix Heguera), Michael Bryan French (Dennis O'Connell), John Prosky (Officer Randall Carlson), Marnie Andrews (Ada Patricia Lyne), Marty Levy (Ed), Robyn Peterson (Marilyn Hopkins), Ray Reinhardt (David Braeder), Lynnie Godfrey (Winona Walker), Robert Gossett (Edward Manley), Jay O. Sanders (Michael Phillips), Mary Alice (Maxine Manley), Michael Chiklis (Jimmy Hoffs), John Hancock (Judge Richard Armand), Concetta Tomei (Susan Hauber), Jenna Cole (Cynthia Brown), Leonard Kibrick (Foreperson), Jenny Manley (Donzaleigh Abernathy), Richard Camphuis (Security Guard #1), Joe Nesnow (Security Guard #2), Darryl Cox (Robert Kurpaska), Milton Murrill (Spectator #1), Keenan Thomas (Spectator #2), Sloan Robinson (Spectator #3), Johnnie Johnson (Spectator #4), Quincy Adams, Jr. (Spectator #5)

Brackman, now cured of his sexual problems, convinces Marilyn to go out with him socially and they have a great time together. A serious relationship starts to develop between them.

Standing before Judge Van Owen is eight-year-old Felix, a crack delivery boy who shot a cop to death because his boss had told him to shoot anyone who tried to take his delivery. The entire situation stuns her, but Van Owen elects to let the boy consider what he has done while restricted to his home, except for school, by an electronic bracelet that will keep authorities informed of his movements. Hopefully this will alter his life for the better. Fe-

lix practically slaps her in the face when he tells her that all of this doesn't mean a damn thing to him.

Rollins represents the Manley family, who charge the Los Angeles Police Department destroyed their home when they mistook it for a crack house. Police officers in charge take the stand and, while they apologize for getting the wrong address, feel they haven't done anything wrong. In fact, if they had to do it again, they would. Neighbors testify they would prefer the police be there, even if an occasional mistake is made, rather than put up with the drug dealers. The Manleys, of course, don't agree. The jury awards the Manleys $43,000, while finding the LAPD innocent of the charges against them.

A riot breaks out in the courtroom, with Judge Conover, the attorneys, plaintiffs and defendants escaping into the judge's chambers. Hours later, Rollins returns to the courtroom to pick up some papers he left behind, and is surprised to find Judge Conover sitting amongst the wreckage that had once been his courtroom. Conover explains that for the first time the outside world truly did invade his courtroom, and it scares him.

Sifuentes is approached by friend Jimmy Hoffs, who is representing Cynthia Brown, wife of a 40-year-old dentist who died of cirrhosis of the liver, despite the fact he had only been a moderate drinker. The suit is against Holstens Blended, makers of the only spirits he drank. Sifuentes agrees to help him out on this situation, believing a larger law firm will help Jimmy make his case.

One of Holstens' lawyers, David Braeder, is an old friend of Rosalind's. He goes to her and offers a settlement of $350,000. If Sifuentes accepts this, the odds are strong that McKenzie-Brackman will get a large part of their

137

business. Later, she suggests that Sifuentes offer the settlement to the client. He refuses, and Rosalind goes to client Cynthia Brown, claiming the only reason Jimmy Hoffs is fighting for her so strongly is that he's after the publicity an issue like this will generate. Adds Rosalind, she would probably be better off taking the settlement.

That afternoon, Sifuentes bursts into Rosalind's office and gets into a major argument with her over the fact that Cynthia fired Jimmy Hoffs. How could she go around him like that? Rosalind warns him to act like a civilized human being in her office or she'll fire him. Sifuentes makes it easy for her. After he finishes his pending cases, he quits!

(The spider woman strikes again, and this time Rosalind Shays has started her own demise at McKenzie-Brackman. This is truly a great confrontation scene, with both Jimmy Smits and Diana Muldaur right on the money in terms of their performances.)

Episode Eighty

"Bang....Zoom....Zap"

Written by David E. Kelley and William M. Finkelstein

Directed Miles Watkins

Guest Stars: James Avery (Judge Michael Conover), Larry Dobkin (Judge Saul Edelstein), Carmen Argenziano (Neil Robertson), Vincent Gardenia (Murray Melman), Michael Ayr (William Sanderland), Elena Stiteler (Ada Ellen Harris), Amber Alexander (Clerk), Chad Taylor (Dr. Leonard), George Pentecost (Joan Nystrom), Jacky DeHaviland (Foreperson), Lance LeGault (Scott Perot), Sal Vecchio (Police Officer), Jeffrey DeMunn (Peter Reynolds), Annie Korzen (Dr. Kravitz), Richard Chaves (Carlos Mendez)

Roxanne's father Murray is kicked out

of a retirement home because he disrupts normal procedure. He continues to slip in and out of a delusion in which he is Ralph Kramden and the person nearest him is abused as though he were Ed Norton. She suggests he move in with her, but he refuses. At episode's end, she has to bail him out of jail because while under the Ralph Kramden fantasy he stole a city bus.

Van Owen punishes a rich doctor who has stolen by sentencing him to two years in prison. Everyone is shocked, but her feeling is that he is a criminal and should be punished as one. The fact that he was wealthy to begin with and felt he had to steal, makes the crime even more serious. Later, Judge Conover, Grace's confidant, has a meeting with her, explaining that her rulings are jamming up the dockets because they're all being appealed. Van Owen is only trying to run her courtroom firmly, but he suggests she use a little common sense. The system is being clogged. During drinks with Kuzak, Van Owen admits that her days as a judge are extremely limited.

When Sifuentes learns that Holstens Companies might become a client, his anger at Rosalind Shays intensifies. He can't believe she cast off a client for the sake of trying to hook a bigger fish. McKenzie discusses this with Rosalind, who claims that Sifuentes wasn't doing right by his client. Holstens possibly becoming a client of the firm's had nothing to do with it. McKenzie lays his cards on the table: he doesn't trust her at all. To make things tougher on him, Kuzak tells McKenzie that his father in New York is sick and he's thinking of relocating.

Recognizing that the firm will collapse if Kuzak leaves, he wants to know if his becoming senior partner again will make a difference. Kuzak isn't so sure, but McKenzie knows what he has to do. He lunches with Scott Perot, CEO of Petramco Industries and tells him that he's thinking of pushing Rosalind out of the senior partner position. Perot doesn't like the idea, saying that he's never been happier with McKenzie-Brackman. McKenzie is shocked, and gets into an argument with Rosalind when she finds out about his meeting with Perot.

Markowitz represents Peter Reynolds, an American living in Argentina during the late 70's and tortured by the military there. At the moment he is suing Carlos Mendez, who inflicted much of the torture he went through. Mendez argues that he was just following orders and had no choice. Markowitz counters that the Nazis used the same argument at Nuremberg, and it just isn't a good enough excuse. If Mendez hated what he was doing, he should have gone AWOL. The decision is in the jury's hands, and they rule in favor of Mendez. Afterward, Mendez apologizes with all his heart and even offers to give Reynolds a job to try and make amends for the past. Reynolds isn't interested. All he wants is revenge. He pulls out a gun and aims it at Mendez. He pulls the trigger, but there are no bullets. Mendez nonetheless breaks down in tears.

Episode Eighty-One

"Forgive Me Father, For I Have Sued"

Written by David E. Kelley and John Romano

Directed by Elodie Keene

Guest Stars: Vincent Gardenia (Murray Melman), Phyllis Lyons (Kate Delahanty), Dick O'Neill (Father Walter McNamara), Stanley Grover (Judge Richard Lobel), Stephen James (Dr. Leonard Smithson), Robert Harper (Brian La Porte), Lillian Lehman (Judge Mary Harcourt), Ray Walston (Gus Nivens), Josie Kim (Clerk), Barbara Beckley (Foreperson), John Diehl (Joseph Delahanty)

Murray Melman is diagnosed as having Alzheimer's Disease and Roxanne pushes to get conservatorship. It's a long struggle, but the judge ultimately agrees because it's obvious that Murray is becoming as much a danger to himself as he is to other people.

McKenzie announces he's going to seek reinstatement as senior partner, which shocks everyone—particularly Rosalind. McKenzie starts pressuring people to vote for him, and even exchanges a promise with Rollins and Abby to push them for partner when the time comes if they side with him. In private, Brackman has a meeting with Kelsey, Kuzak, Markowitz and Becker to spell out the dilemma they're in: if Rosalind leaves the firm, she will take her clients with her and the partners could be in serious financial trouble.

At a subsequent meeting, the partners tell Rosalind their complaints, but she comes up with an excuse for each of them, adding that if she leaves the firm, nearly 50 percent of the clients will go with her. McKenzie delivers a speech about the way he built the company on loyalty and with a feeling of family. Rosalind discusses things from her point of view, which is mostly business. Before the final vote can be taken, Rosalind steps down as senior partner and resigns.

Sifuentes represents Father McNamara, who is being sued by Kevin Delahanty. His wife is an emotional wreck, because McNamara will not absolve her of the sin of using birth control during sex as he has done for the past couple of years. McNamara no longer believes that she truly means to repent. Being extremely religious, she honestly feels that the lack of absolution will condemn her soul to the pits of hell for all eternity. For this reason, she won't come near her husband or her children. McNamara feels he can't change the law of the church, even though it has become more lenient in recent years.

The jury deliberates for a short time and awards Delahanty $250,000. The man tells Sifuentes that he doesn't want the money, just his wife back. Sifuentes talks to the priest about this, emphasizing that Mrs. Delahanty is obviously sorry for what she's done by the fact she has avoided sex for so long. He considers this and then goes to absolve her.

(NOTE: Character actor Dick O'Neill (Father McNamara) portrayed Charlie Cagney on the television series Cagney and Lacey.*)*

Episode Eighty-Two

"Outward Bound"

Written by David E. Kelley and William M. Finkelstein

Directed by Ed Sherin

Guest Stars: Sheila Kelley (Gwen), Lindsay Crouse (Sharon Cummings), Maryann Plunkett (Theresa Cavanaugh), Warren Munson (Judge Matthew Saucier), Michael Medeiros (Stan Vlasic), Nicolas Surovy (Warren Smyth), Jennifer Hetrick (Corrinne Hammond), Amanda Plummer (Alice Hackett), Wayne Tippit (Leo Hackett), Craig Wasson (Tom Cavanaugh), Ashleigh Sterling (Chloe Hammond), Judy Kain (Joanna), Kate Benton (Sara), Megan Parlen (Little Girl), Tony Cannata (Foreperson)

Benny is performing in a local production of *The Wizard of Oz* as The Cowardly Lion, while Alice portrays Dorothy. He is shocked to find her kissing the actor playing Scarecrow and decides that he no longer wants to marry her. She tries to make up with him, but Benny knocks her to the floor, bruising her face. Sifuentes yells at him, and Leo Hackett has a serious talk with him about losing his temper like that. At a restaurant, Benny says he only wants her to kiss him and no longer wants to get married. Alice is crushed, but has no choice but to accept this.

Becker proposes to Corrinne, but ends up having an affair with his temporary secretary, Gwen. Roxanne realizes what went on and scolds him for it but, as is her wont, tries to understand him.

During a staff meeting, McKenzie says Rosalind will be leaving the firm by the end of the week. Kuzak announces he is going to relocate to New York to be closer to his father. Later, he tells McKenzie that he's not sure he'll be returning, because this just isn't the same place it once was. Needing to fill the void quickly, McKenzie turns to Grace Van Owen, who plans on leaving her judgeship. When McKenzie agrees to her terms, including being made the head of litigation, she tells him she'll sign on. At episode's end there is a moment where everyone welcomes Grace as Rosalind walks through the doors alone. You can't help but feel a wee bit of sympathy for ole Ros.

Kuzak represents former police officer Tom Cavanaugh, forced to resign when journalist Warren Smyth wrote an article that exposed the fact he is gay. Cavanaugh preferred to hide his sexual preferences, but Smyth's attorney, Sharon Cummings, tries to convince the jury—and maybe even Cavanaugh himself—that living a lie for 20 years has caused him more pain than the truth ever could. Because Cavanaugh was a hero cop, she reasons, he became "public property", and fearful homosexuals could look to him as an example. Kuzak proves that Cavanaugh's personal and public life has become hell since Smyth's article ran, and that like all Americans he's entitled to his privacy. The jury finds for Cavanaugh. After the trial, Smyth offers a hand of friendship to Cavanaugh. That hand is rejected.

Episode Eighty-Three

"The Last Gasp"

Written by David E. Kelley and William M. Finkelstein

Directed by Rick Wallace

Guest Stars: Renee Jones (Diana Moses), Robyn Peterson (Marilyn Hopkins), Kate Benton (Sara), Jeanne Cooper (Gladys Becker), Ashleigh Sterling (Chloe Hammond), Michael Laskin (Judge Mark London), Laura Austin (Carrie), Jennifer Hetrick (Corrinne Hammond), Mike Ditka (Himself), Henry G. Sanders (Judge Andrew Robertson), A. Martinez (Hector Rodriguez), John Kapelos (Jack Lewis), Sheila Kelley (Gwen), Peter Van Norden (Allard Keene), William Jordan (Mark Johnson), Jerry Hardin (D.A. Malcolm Gold), Mike Nussbaum (Henry Sutter), Nancy Sheeber (Foreperson), George Coe (Judge Wallace R. Vance), Joseph Medalis (Federal Judge Jackson), Harry Rhodes (Federal Judge Emmanuel), Darlene Kardon (Federal Judge Constance Greg), John Pleshette (Mark Kumpel), Carmen Zapzta (Irene Rodriguez), Terry L. Beaver (Norman Patton), Laurie Souza (Maria Rodriguez), Bill Lee Brown (Clerk), Opin Kennedy (Reporter #1), Tina Panella-Hart (Reporter #2), Kim Murdock (Reporter #3), Alec Murdock (Reporter #4), Frank Birney (The Warden), Mik Scriba (Bob, the Guard)

In a humorous court case, Kelsey defends the Chicago Bears football team against irate fan Jack Lewis, who claims the Bears lied in their preseason boast of a great team that would be headed for the Super Bowl. He wants the money back that he spent on a satellite dish to watch the games, plus damages for the emotional pressure the team put him through. Things are settled when the judge orders Lewis to air his anger at team coach Mike Ditka, and one can be sure that the man has a lot to say.

Becker announces that he will be getting married at the end of the week, and much to everyone's surprise, he actually goes through with it.

Van Owen, in her first McKenzie-Brackman case, represents 70-year-old Henry Sutter in the mercy killing of his wife, who was dying of Alzheimer's Disease. The man wants a not-guilty verdict rather than being jailed for two years under a manslaughter charge. Opposing counsel Malcolm Gold quickly puts down Sutter's temporary insanity plea and despite Van Owen's best efforts, the jury finds him guilty of second-degree murder. He will go to jail.

Kuzak tells Van Owen his father has decided to move to Los Angeles, so Kuzak will no longer have to go East. The question is, can he and Van Owen work in the same office while leading their own private lives? Only time will tell.

Sifuentes, now remaining with the firm, takes on the case of an old childhood friend named Hector Rodriguez, who has been sentenced to die in the gas chamber for murder. Desperately, Sifuentes tries to get a stay from the governor but his efforts are futile. Rodriguez, who realizes he's going to die, asks Victor to be there and it's a request Sifuentes reluctantly honors. Once again, Jimmy Smits does an incredible job as he watches an old friend die.

Thus ends the fourth season of *L.A. Law*—one which truly shook things up for the partners and associates and the pieces of which would not hit the ground until season five.

SEASON FIVE

(AS OF 12/90)

PRODUCTION STAFF

Executive Producer: David E. Kelley
Co-Executive Producer: Rick Wallace
Producer: John Hill
Producer: James C. Hart
Producer: Elodie Keene
Producer: Patricia Green
Producer: Robert M. Breech
Coordinating Producer: Alice West

REGULAR CAST

Harry Hamlin: Michael Kuzak
Susan Dey: Grace Van Owen
Corbin Bernsen: Arnold Becker
Jill Eikenberry: Ann Kelsey
Alan Rachins: Douglas Brackman, Jr.
Michele Greene: Abby Perkins
Jimmy Smits: Victor Sifuentes
Michael Tucker: Stuart Markowitz
Susan Ruttan: Roxanne Melman
Richard Dysart: Leland McKenzie
Blair Underwood: Jonathan Rollins
Larry Drake: Benny Stulwicz
Amanda Donohoe: C.J. Lamb
John Spencer: Tommy Mullaney

Episode Eighty-Four

"The Bitch is Back"

Written by David E. Kelley

Directed by Elodie Keene

Guest Stars: Vincent Gardenia (Murray Melman), Diana Muldaur (Rosalind Shays), Dennis Arndt (Jack Sollers), Anne Haney (Judge Marilyn Travelini), Bruce Kirby (D.A. Bruce Rogoff), Francois Giroday (Dr. Jeffrie Wolin), Jordan Baker (Marcia Fusco), Jennifer Hetrick (Corrinne Hammond Becker), Dan Moseley (Police Officer), Ashley Sterling (Chloe Hammond Becker), Hiram Kasten (Kenny Alder), Tina Panella-Hart (Reporter #1), Orin Kennedy (Reporter #3), Alec Murdock (Reporter #2), Charles Bazaldua (Foreperson), J. Kenneth Campbell (Judge Walter Stone), Tim Guinee (Brian Chisolm), Paul Winfield (Derron Holloway), Chauncy Leopardi (Eric Perkins)

In the tradition of the Earl Williams trial, Kuzak begins another long one, this time involving a white police officer named Brian Chisolm who accidentally shot and killed a black youth. Now, black activist Derron Holloway (who New Yorkers may recognize as a thinly veiled Reverend Al Sharpton) is stirring up the media, intensifying the racial aspect of the case.

The prosecution offers an involuntary manslaughter charge which will result in Chisolm losing his job, but all the media attention has caused the offer to be withdrawn. Kuzak tries desperately to get the plea bargain, but he is refused. Despite Rollins' opposition, Kuzak wants him to serve as second chair on the case, hoping that his involvement will alleviate some of the media pressure.

Rosalind Shays sues McKenzie-Brackman over being fired, and the damage to her reputation that it caused. The settlement fee is $500,000, but the firm would rather fight. Since Sifuentes and Van Owen are the two people not mentioned in the suit, they are the ones providing defense. Rosalind's lawyer, Jack Sollers, starts off attacking McKenzie-Brackman as a group of incompetents who needed Rosalind Shays to save their firm, and then kicked her out once she gave them exactly what they wanted.

Markowitz is unexpectedly put on the stand and he does so poorly that in private it begins a wave of arguments that end when he suffers a heart attack and is rushed to the hospital. Soon thereafter he is sent home to rest. Back in court, Rosalind takes the stand and gives quite a performance as the poor good girl taken advantage of and thrown out with the trash. Van Owen moves to attack Rosalind on a personal level, emphasizing how she creates friction wherever she goes; that she is a woman incapable of maintaining a friendship with anyone, including her own daughter and grandchildren.

That is the reason she was asked to step down as senior partner and not because they were through with her. Simply put, she had cultivated no loyalty amongst the partners. Jack Sollers calls Kelsey to the stand and has her recall a conversation she had with Rosalind in which she said that had Ros been a man, she would have been heralded as a great hero, but a woman is treated differently. This seems to be the final nail in McKenzie's defense.

(NOTE: Things are certainly off to an interesting start, and Diana Muldaur is a wonder to behold as she manages to wriggle her character out of every charge that is levelled against her. It's also of interest to see McKenzie lose his cool the way he does, emphasizing more and more that he isn't the perfect saint the audience might have thought him to be during the first couple of seasons. Overall it lends a sense of realism to the proceedings.)

Episode Eighty-Five

"Happy Trails"

Written by David E. Kelley

Directed by Win Phelps

Guest Stars: Vincent Gardenia (Murray Melman), Diana Muldaur (Rosalind Shays), Dennis Arndt (Jack Sollers), Anne Haney (Judge Marilyn Travelini), Jordan Baker (Marcia Fusco), Charles Bazaldua (Foreperson), J. Kenneth Campbell (Judge Walter Stone), Tim Guinee (Brian Chisolm), Paul Winfield (Derron Holloway), Sheila Kelley (Gwen Taylor), Kate Finlayson (Reporter #4), Robyn Peterson (Marilyn Hopkins), Kristina Coggins (Susan Raab), Duane Davis (Arthur Pryor), Tim Hart (Waiter), Monica Horan (Reporter #1), Hector Maisonette (Rudy Lewis), Randy Broad (Reporter #2), Jonathan Doll (Reporter #3), Barry Pintar (Anchorman), Steve Small (Bailiff #1), William Finkelstein (Howard Hulce), Darwyn Carson (Bailiff #2)

Brackman goes to see Marilyn and is shocked to see some of the depraved clients she deals with. It's more than he can stand and he breaks off the relationship, although she fights to keep it going.

(NOTE: If one has a complaint about this story point, it's that the writers suddenly turn Marilyn into a hooker rather than a sex therapist, and it's a disturbing change. The character's class is suddenly taken away from her, and that's unfortunate, as she and Brackman played off each other nicely.)

The Rosalind Shays trial continues, with Jack Sollers hitting members of McKenzie-Brackman as hard as he can, and Van Owen returning the favor to Rosalind. In closing arguments, Sollers argues that Rosalind has been mistreated and abused simply because she is a woman. Van Owen counters that the jury should feel pity for Rosalind Shays and her inability to maintain a relationship, but that they must realize that she was not wronged in this situation. No one asked her to leave the firm. She did this on her own. The jury deliberates and finds for Rosalind, awarding her one dollar in compensatory damages. Punitive damages, however, are in the amount of $2.1 million.

Derron Holloway continues the media frenzy surrounding Kuzak's case, and the lawyer's frustration only mounts when he feels that Judge Walter Stone is being so carefully political that he's biased against him. Kuzak recommends that Stone excuse himself from the trial, but he refuses to do so. Desperate to get more time for this trial, Kuzak tells Stone that Chisolm is unhappy with his representation and wants a new lawyer.

Stone accepts this but states that the trial will go on as scheduled, with Rollins serving as the police officer's attorney. That idea ruined, Kuzak turns to Holloway and offers a civil claim in the case provided that the man stop talking to the press, but Holloway won't have anything to do with such a move.

As the trial begins, Kuzak insults Stone by calling him a chicken S.O.B. He's held in contempt of court and taken away. Stone insists that Rollins pick up where Kuzak left off and Jonathan says, "I think he called you a chicken S.O.B. But he forgot to mention that you're stupid, and. . . ." Stone has Rollins taken away as well, and has no choice but to declare a mistrial.

Episode Eighty-Six

"Lie Harder"

Written by David E. Kelley

Directed by David Carson

Guest Stars: Paul Winfield (Derron Holloway), Jennifer Hetrick (Corrinne Becker), Diana Muldaur (Rosalind Shays), Dennis Arndt (Jack Sollers), Castulo Guerra (Jaime Fodriguez), Anne Haney (Judge Marilyn Travelini), C.C.H. Pounder (Judge Roseann Robin), Bruce Kirby (Bruce Rogoff), Sheila Kelley (Gwen Taylor), John Hancock (Judge Richard Armand), Tim Guinee (Brian Chisolm), Jordan Baker (Marcia Fusco), James Avery (Judge Michael Conover), Thomas C. Morgan (Jerome Bailey), Gay Hagen (Jury Foreperson), Chauncey Leopardi (Eric Perkins), Paul Eiding (Ben Slaeffer), Christine Jansen (Carol Slaeffer), Dan Cashman (Mr. Lowry), Jenny O'Hara (Dr. Sarah Evans), John Christina Graas (Billy Slaeffer), Marian Green (Amy Lewis)

Becker's pre-marriage fling, Gwen, is now working for Markowitz and it turns out that she and his wife, Corrinne, are old friends who rediscover each other. Becker is horrified and desperate to get Gwen out of there, so he tells Markowitz that he ought to be careful of her, because she hit on him the week before he got married. This little statement eventually reaches Gwen who bursts into Arnie's office and tells him off, though she doesn't mention anything to Corrinne.

McKenzie meets with Rosalind to try to work out a more amicable settlement, and she eventually settles for $1.4 million. We also get the first sense of a friendship and respect between them. As Sollers and Van Owen sign the settlement papers, he asks her out to dinner and she accepts.

In a heart-wrenching story, Abby represents the Slaeffer family, which wants to return an adopted child because he is so emotionally disturbed. They've tried to work out the problems on their own, but now the boy is actually injuring other members of the family and the parents fear that some day it could re-

sult in one of them being killed. The Department of Social Services tries to argue against this, declaring they can't start implementing a system by which every parent unhappy with adopted children can return them with no questions asked. While Judge Robin agrees with this sentiment, there doesn't seem to be any choice in returning young Billy to the adoption agency. He is indeed a threat.

(NOTE: The final scene in which Billy is taken away from his parents breaks your heart. The parents don't really want to give him up because they have grown to love him, and Billy definitely wants to stay with them. Your eyes fill up as Billy pleads, "I'll be good. Let me come home mommy and daddy. I promise, I'll be good!" Whew.)

Assistant District Attorney Fusco has found a witness in the Chisolm shooting case, which stuns Kuzak. Holloway held a town meeting and asked any witnesses to step forward and this boy did. Shortly thereafter, Van Owen is able to convince Judge Conover to replace Judge Stone on the case, as she considers Conover to be one of the fairest judges she knows. Conover asks to see the young Bailey, who is the supposed witness, and finds his testimony to be strong enough that it does warrant a trial. Both Conover and Kuzak are less than happy when it turns out that Holloway is Bailey's lawyer, but Conover quickly puts the man in his place before they take another step forward.

Episode Eighty-Seven

"Armand's Hammer"

Directed by Menachem Binetski

Guest Stars: Paul Winfield (Derron Holloway), Dennis Arndt (Jack Sollers), John Harkins (Martin Lowens), John Hancock (Judge Richard Armand), Tim Guinee (Brian Chisolm), Jordan Baker (Marcia Fusco), Raye

Birk (Judge Steven Lang), Barry Snider (August Oberzan), Gay Hagen (Foreperson), Vernee Watson-Johnson (Wilma Russ), John Vickery (Kenneth Clipner), Thomas C. Morgan (Jerome Bailey), Redmond M. Gleeson (Foreman), Kandis Chappell (Gail Egan), Ernie Orsatti (Utility Stunt)

Sifuentes represents Martin Lowens, who is suing the producers of *America's Most Embarrassing Practical Jokes* for lifting his toupee while on national television. He originally thought he was taping an editorial response and didn't feel the fishing hooks that lifted his toupee. In fact, he didn't know it had happened at all until it went on the air. As a result, he lost his job. The videotape is shown in court and it's difficult for the jurors and those in attendance to stifle their laughter. Lowens uses this to his advantage by delivering his own closing argument and stating that although the video is indeed funny, it has hurt his personal and professional life badly. The jury awards him $45,000.

In the Chisolm case, Holloway puts Jerome Bailey on the stand, and the youth claims to have seen Chisolm shoot the victim when no one else was around. What Rollins wants to know is why Bailey never told anyone about this, not even his friends or his mother. Maybe it's because he never saw anything and is merely coming forward because he's been told to do so.

During a break, Rollins approaches Holloway and discusses the way that the man is destroying the legal system by turning everything into a racial issue. Holloway responds with the simple fact that this case would never have gone to trial if not for him. When court reconvenes, Chisolm takes the stand and explains that two men shot at him from the other end of an alley and he returned fire. Yes, he did shoot the victim, but it was an honest accident. Fusco tries to make Chisolm out to be a racist who killed the victim on purpose.

Rollins manages to get Holloway up on the stand and admit that because Chisolm was white and the victim black, he assumed it was murder. Would Holloway be involved if the victim was white? No. Then maybe Holloway is a racist. The jury considers all they have heard and come back with a verdict of murder in the second degree. Holloway is overjoyed, until Judge Conover stops the celebration.

With the evidence presented, there is simply no way that the jury should have found Chisolm guilty. Due to the fact that they allowed the grandstanding surrounding the case to influence them, they didn't fulfill their collective duty as a jury. Conover overturns the verdict and declares Chisolm not guilty.

(NOTE: In these first four episodes, we can see the fifth season get off to a tremendous start, wrapping up leftover plotlines and beginning new ones. The idea of doing story arcs over the course of several episodes is wonderful, truly giving the show's creative team the opportunity to explore larger themes. At this point L.A. Law is five years old, but it seems as fresh today as when it premiered, and that is the quality that will allow the series to stand the test of time.)

Secretary Roxanne Melman, portrayed by Susan Ruttan, is not about to take any nonsense from her boss, lawyer Arnie Becker, portrayed by Corbin Bernsen

RECOGNITION

LA LAW has been widely recognized by viewers, critics and industry as one of the finest drama series ever broadcast. The show has piled up quite a stack of Emmy nominations and awards.

Victor Sifuentes, portrayed by Emmy nominee Jimmy Smits (left) consults the firm's patriarch, founding partner Leland McKenzie, portrayed by Richard Dysart.

1986-1987 FIRST SEASON

11/10/86: Electronic Media Survey, included on "The Best Shows" List

1/31/87: Golden Globe Awards, Best Drama Series

3/15/87: People's Choice Awards, Favorite New Television Dramatic Program

5/15/87: BMI Motion Picture and Television Awards, Honored with Television Music Award

5/16/87: Electronic Media Poll, Included on "Best Regular Series" List

6/1/87: People Magazine, Harry Hamlin voted "Sexiest Man Alive" for 1987

6/17/87: Imagen Awards, Imagen Recognition Award—"Raiders of the Lost Bark"

9/20/87: Emmy Awards

Outstanding Drama Series—Steven Bochco, Executive Producer; Gregory Hoblit, Co-Executive Producer; Terry Louise Fisher, Supervising Producer; Ellen S. Pressman, Scott Goldstein, Producers; Phillip M. Goldfarb, Coordinating Producer

Outstanding Writing in a Drama Series– Steven Bochco, Terry Louise Fisher for "Venus Butterfly"

Outstanding Directing in a Drama Series– Gregory Hoblit for "Pilot"

Outstanding Guest Performer in a Drama Series– Alfre Woodard (Adrian Moore)

Outstanding Art Direction for a Series– Jeffrey L. Goldstein, Production Designer; Richard K. Kent, Set Director. Both for "Pilot"

11/10/87: Women at Work Broadcast Awards, First Place—Entertainment for "Raiders of the Lost Bark"

2/10/87: Alliance of Gay and Lesbian Artists, "The Venus Butterfly" honored for "responsible portrayal of gay and lesbian characters and issues in entertainment media."

7/17/87: Nosotros Golden Eagle Award, Jimmy Smits—"Outstanding Actor in a TV Series"

7/30/87: Television Critics Award, TCA Award for Excellence in Drama

8/27/87: Kodak, Eastman Award for Excellence to Robert Seaman for "Outstanding Contribution to the Art of Cinematography"

10/28/87: Casting Society of America, Dramatic Episodic Casting category; Nan Dutton (Casting Director) for "Pilot"

12/8/87: Electronic Media Survey, *L.A. Law* is Number One in Electronic Media's "Annual Survey"

Michael Tucker portrays Stuart Markowitz, a tax-whiz lawyer whose cool head often prevails when legal battles mount.

Ann Kelsey, portrayed by Jill Eikenberry, juggles marriage, a child and a demanding legal career.

1987-1988
SECOND SEASON

1/23/88:Golden Globe Awards, Best Television Series (Drama); Susan Dey—Best Performance by an Actress in a Dramatic Series

2/25/88:Association for Retarded Citizens of the U.S., The Association selected the show for its creation and development of the character of Benny Stulwicz—for a commendation in recognition of the show as a positive force for better public understanding of people with mental retardation.

3/13/88:People's Choice Awards, Favorite Dramatic Television Series

4/12/88:Council for Exceptional Children, Honored with NBC for the inspirational depiction of the character of Benny Stulwicz

5/3/88: Electronic Media Poll, Favorite show among the nation's TV critics

5/4/88:George Foster Peabody Award

6/16/88:Imagen Awards, Special Recognition Award

8/28/88: Emmy Awards

Outstanding Supporting Actor in a Dramatic Series– Larry Drake as Benny Stulwicz

Outstanding Editing for a Dramatic Series (Single Camera Production)— Elodie Keene for "Full Marital Jacket"

12/13/88:Women at Work Broadcast Awards, Entertainment Category—Second Place for "Beauty and Obese"

12/27/88:Television Theme Music Awards, "Music From L.A. Law and Otherwise;" Mike Post, Best Record Release

1988-1989
THIRD SEASON

1/22/89:Media Access Awards, Special Merit for "Benny Stulwicz" character

1/28/89:Golden Globe Awards, Jill Eikenberry—Best Performance by an Actress in a Television Series

2/22/89:Grammy Awards, Music from "L.A. Law"—Mike Post

3/12/89:People's Choice Awards, Favorite Television Dramatic Series

6/15/89:Imagen Award, Special Recognition Award

9/17/89:Emmy Awards

Raising a toast at McKenzie, Brackman, Chaney and Kuzak are (left) Blair Underwood, Michele Greene and Jimmy Smits.

Outstanding Supporting Actor in a Dramatic Series— Larry Drake for Benny Stulwicz character

Outstanding Dramatic Series

11/9/89:Channels Magazine, Steven Bochco—Excellence in Television Award

1989-1990 FOURTH SEASON

2/11/90:Genesis Awards, Outstanding Television Dramatic Series

2/11/90:Director's Guild Awards, Best Dramatic Series—Night Category; Eric Laneuville, "I'm in the Nude for Love"

3/11/90:People Choice Awards, Favorite Dramatic Television Series

4/29/90:GLAAD Media Awards, Best Depiction of Gay/Lesbian dilemma

6/10/90:Blanche Rosloff Good Neighbor Award/Westside Fair Housing Council, Best Depiction of fighting bigotry and discrimination—"Watts a Matter," David E. Kelley and Bryce Zabel, writers

7/26/90:Viewers for Quality Television Nomination, Jimmy Smits—Best Supporting Actor, Quality Drama

9/18/90:Emmy Awards

Best Dramatic Series

Best Actor in a Drama Series, Jimmy Smits for the character Victor Sifuentes

Boring, But Necessary Ordering Information!

Payment:

All orders must be prepaid by check or money order. Do not send cash. All payments must be made in US funds only.

Shipping:

We offer several methods of shipment for our product. Sometimes a book can be delayed if we are temporarily out of stock. You should note on your order whether you prefer us to ship the book as soon as available or send you a merchandise credit good for other goodies or send you your money back immediately.

Postage is as follows:

Normal Post Office: For books priced under $10.00—for the first book add $2.50. For each additional book under $10.00 add $1.00. (This is per indidividual book priced under $10.00. Not the order total.) For books priced over $10.00—for the first book add $3.25. For each additional book over $10.00 add $2.00.(This is per individual book priced over $10.00, not the order total.) These orders are filled as quickly as possible. Shipments normally take 2 or 3 weeks, but allow up to 12 weeks for delivery.

Special UPS 2 Day Blue Label Rush Service or Priority Mail(Our Choice). Special service is available for desperate Couch Potatoes. These books are shipped within 24 hours of when we receive the order and should normally take 2 to 3 days to get from us to you.

For the first RUSH SERVICE book under $10.00 add $5.00. For each additional 1 book under $10.00 add $1.75. (This is per individual book priced under $10.00, not the order total.)

For the first RUSH SERVICE book over $10.00 add $7.00 For each additional book over $10.00 add $4.00 per book.(This is per individual book priced over $10.00, not the order total.)

Canadian shipping rates add 20% to the postage total.
Foreign shipping rates add 50% to the postage total.

All Canadian and foreign orders are shipped either book or printed matter.
Rush Service is not available.

DISCOUNTS!DISCOUNTS!

Because your orders keep us in business we offer a discount to people that buy a lot of our books as our way of saying thanks. On orders over $25,00 we give a 5% discount. On orders over $50.00 we give a 10% discount. On orders over $100.00 we give a 15% discount. On orders over over $150.00 we giver a 20 % discount.

Please list alternates when possible.

Please state if you wish a refund or for us to backorder an item if it is not in stock.

100% satisfaction guaranteed.

We value your support. You will receive a full refund as long as the copy of the book you are not happy with is received back by us in reasonable condition. No questions asked, except we would like to know how we failed you. Refunds and credits are given as soon as we receive back the item you do not want.

Please have mercy on Phyllis and carefully fill out this form in the neatest way you can. Remember, she has to read a lot of them every day and she wants to get it right and keep you happy! You may use a duplicate of this order blank as long as it is clear. Please don't forget to include payment! And remember, we love repeat friends.

COUPON PAGE

_____Secret File: The Unofficial Making Of A Wiseguy $14.95 ISBN # 1-55698-256-9

_____Number Six: The Prisoner Book $14.95   ISBN# 1-55698-158-9

_____Gerry Anderson: Supermarionation $14.95

_____Calling Tracy $14.95 ISBN# 1-55698-241-0

_____How To Draw Art For Comicbooks: Lessons From The Masters

                                                        ISBN# 1-55698-254-2

_____The 25th Anniversary Odd Couple Companion $12.95   ISBN# 1-55698-224-0

_____Growing up in The Sixties: The wonder Years $14.95   ISBN #1-55698-258-5

_____Batmania $14.95   ISBN# 1-55698-252-6

_____The Year Of The Bat $14.95

_____The King Comic Heroes $14.95

_____Its A Bird, Its A Plane $14.95   ISBN# 1-55698-201-1

_____The Green Hornet Book $14.95

_____The Green Hornet Book $16.95 Edition

_____The Unofficial Tale Of Beauty And The Beast $14.95   ISBN# 1-55698-261-5

_____Monsterland Fear Book $14.95

_____Nightmare On Elm Street: The Freddy Krueger Story $14.95

_____Robocop $16.95

_____The Aliens Story $14.95

_____The Dark Shadows Tribute Book $14.95   ISBN#1-55698-234-8

_____Stephen King & Clive Barker: An Illustrated Guide $14.95 ISBN#1-55698-253-4

_____Drug Wars: America fights Back $9.95 ISBN#1-55698-259-3

_____The Films Of Elvis: The Magic Lives On $14.95   ISBN#1-55698-223-2

_____Paul McCartney: 20 Years On His Own $9.95   ISBN#1-55698-263-1

_____Fists Of Fury: The Films Of Bruce Lee $14.95   ISBN# 1-55698-233-X

_____The Secret Of Michael F Fox $14.95   ISBN# 1-55698-232-1

_____The Films Of Eddie Murphy $14.95   ISBN# 1-55698-230-5

_____The Lost In Space Tribute Book $14.95   ISBN# 1-55698-226-7

_____The Lost In Space Technical Manual $14.95

_____Doctor Who: The Pertwee Years $19.95   ISBN#1-55698-212-7

_____Doctor Who: The Baker Years $19.95   ISBN# 1-55698-147-3

_____The Doctor Who Encyclopedia: The Baker Years $19.95   ISBN# 1-55698-160-0

_____The Doctor And The Enterprise $9.95   ISBN# 1-55698-218-6

_____The Phantom Serials $16.95

_____Batman Serials $16.95

MORE COUPON PAGE

_____Batman And Robin Serials $16.95

_____The Complete Batman And Robin Serials $19.95

_____The Green Hornet Serials $16.95

_____The Flash Gordon Serials Part 1 $16.95

_____The Flash Gordon Serials Part 2 $16.95

_____The Shadow Serials $16.95

_____Blackhawk Serials $16.95

_____Serial Adventures $14.95   ISBN#1-55698-236-4

_____Trek: The Lost Years $12.95   ISBN#1-55698-220-8

_____The Trek Encyclopedia $19.95   ISBN#1-55698-205-4

_____The Trek Crew Book $9.95   ISBN#1-55698-257-7

_____The Making Of The Next Generation $14.95   ISBN# 1-55698-219-4

_____The Complete Guide To The Next Generation $19.95

_____The Best Of Enterprise Incidents: The Magazine For Star Trek Fans $9.95
                                              ISBN# 1-55698-231-3

_____The Gunsmoke Years $14.95   ISBN# 1-55698-221-6

_____The Wild Wild West Book $14.95   ISBN# 1-55698-162-7

_____Who Was That Masked Man $14.95   ISBN#1-55698-227-5

NAME:_____

STREET:_____

CITY:_____

STATE:_____

ZIP:_____

TOTAL:_____ SHIPPING_____

SEND TO: Couch Potato, Inc. 5715 N. Balsam Rd., Las Vegas, NV 89130

· COMING ATTRACTIONS ·

_____Top Gun : The Films Of Tom Cruise $14.95

_____Encyclopedia Of Cartoon Superstars $14.95

_____The Films Of Harrison Ford $14.95

_____Sinatrivia $9.95

_____How To Build Models $14.95

_____The Fab Films Of The Beatles $14.95

_____New Kids On The Block $9.95

_____Swashbucklers $14.95

_____Happy Days Companion $14.95

_____Trek Fans Handbook $9.95

_____The Green Hornet Book: Revised And Updated $14.95

_____Rocky And The Films Of Sylvester Stallone $14.95

_____Santa Cat $9.95

NAME:_____

STREET:_____

CITY:_____

STATE:_____

ZIP:_____

TOTAL:_____ SHIPPING_____

SEND TO: Couch Potato, Inc. 5715 N. Balsam Rd., Las Vegas, NV 89130